Penguin Education

Penguin Modern Psychology
General Editor: B. M. Foss

Social Psychology
Editor: M. Argyle

Language and Social Behaviour
W. P. Robinson

W. P. Robinson

Language and Social Behaviour

Penguin Education

Penguin Education
A Division of Penguin Books Ltd,
Harmondsworth, Middlesex, England
Penguin Books Inc, 7110 Ambassador Road,
Baltimore, Md 21207, USA
Penguin Books Australia Ltd,
Ringwood, Victoria, Australia
Penguin Books Canada Ltd,
41 Steelcase Road West,
Markham, Ontario, Canada

First published 1972
Reprinted 1974
Copyright © W. P. Robinson, 1972

Made and printed in Great Britain by
Cox & Wyman Ltd,
London, Reading and Fakenham
Set in Monotype Times

To Susan Rackstraw

Contents

4 Characteristics of Emitter: Marking of Emotional States 80

5 Characteristics of Emitter: Marking of Personality and Social Identity 93

6 Marking of Role Relationships 118

12 Contents

Editorial Foreword

This volume is in the social psychology section of the Penguin Modern Psychology series. In this part of the series a number of volumes are planned which will give a comprehensive coverage of social psychology, each written by active research workers, and providing up-to-date and rigorous accounts of different parts of this subject. There has been an explosive growth of research in social psychology in recent years, and the subject has broken out of its early preoccupation with the laboratory to study social behaviour in a variety of social settings. These volumes will differ somewhat from most existing textbooks: in addition to citing laboratory experiments they will cite field studies, and deal with the details and complexities of the phenomena as they occur in the outside world. Links will be established with other disciplines such as sociology, anthropology, animal behaviour, linguistics, and other branches of psychology, where relevant. As well as being useful to students, these monographs should therefore be of interest to a wider public – those concerned with the various fields dealt with.

This book is about a new field of psychology, sometimes known as 'social psycho-linguistics', or 'the social psychology of language'. Social psychologists have only recently become aware that most human social behaviour involves speech, and research workers have become very interested in the social psychological processes involved. Similarly linguists have become aware that language is used in social situations, to communicate in a number of different ways. Sociologists have become interested in the different ways that language is used in different social classes and cultures.

Peter Robinson is one of the leading research workers in

this field. He has carried out some very sophisticated investigations of class differences in the use of language, and has devised a new scheme for classifying utterances which goes far beyond the methods used in linguistics and has proved very useful for research purposes. He has produced an extremely well-informed and critical book about this new field.

Preface

The brief undertaken was to achieve a perspective that might prove to be a useful framework for the study of the relationships between language and social behaviour and to show how this perspective could be applied to recent, current and perhaps future, work in this field.

If the objective had been to review the literature extant, a number of differences would have resulted. Studies not mentioned would have been, while some of those which are mentioned would not have been given the extended treatment accorded to them here. Not so many questions would have been raised and then left unanswered; the emphasis would have been more heavily on what has been done, as opposed to what has not. There might have been an apparently more ready acceptance of the usefulness of certain lines of inquiry and a lesser concern with worries about methodological problems of ends and means.

The format adopted deliberately attempts to expose gaps and weaknesses in our activities, but the intention has been to be optimistic and constructive about these.

I am pleased to thank Michael Argyle and Elizabeth Peill for their critical reading of drafts of the manuscript and Susan Rackstraw for her suggestions and criticisms. I am grateful to Miss D. Marshallsay for help with preparing the index and Mrs Nunn for typing so efficiently and graciously.

1 Introduction

Behavioural scientists are a favoured target for comedians, both professional and amateur. It may well be that the jokes spring in part from unconscious fears about our potential power over the destiny of mankind, but it also happens that we encourage such humour when we appear to be asking naïve or stupid questions, and occasionally when we make discoveries which fail to set the world alight with surprise and admiration. One of the more profound insights we have achieved since 1945 has been the realization that man speaks. He also listens to speech. Some men read and write as well.

The outside world has not sat back on its heels gasping with amazement at this astonishing discovery, but within the ivory towers of the human section of the behavioural sciences there has been a rapid growth in the number of people studying language and verbal behaviour, a growth which currently shows little sign of abating. New words and phrases have been added to the language. There are now psycholinguists, sociolinguists and, towering above both, syllabically at least, the ethnographers of communication. The first emerged in the 1950s, while persons who are prepared to classify themselves under the last heading may still be counted on only a few handfuls of fingers. If the original version of this book had been delivered on time to the publishers it could have been the first to carry the title 'Sociolinguistics'. As it is, the scope has been narrowed too far, and the focus shifted to include aspects of verbal behaviour outside the purely linguistic, to allow such a title.

The newness of the field carries both advantages and disadvantages. One two-edged advantage is that the amateur may quickly achieve expert status since there is no great body of agglomerated knowledge to absorb. Disadvantages are numerous. Anything written in the field is likely to date very fast, not only because new factual information will accumulate quickly, but also because it is likely that the theoretical frameworks in which this knowledge is held will change. The language(s) linguists use to talk about language has changed very drastically in the last fifteen years and will probably shift again in the very near future. Shifts in framework, or paradigm as Kuhn (1962) calls it, will lead to shifts in what is considered relevant and interesting as well. Anybody who has tried to keep abreast of the state of 'generative grammar' may well have discovered that just before he had mastered Mark I, Mark II arrived, and so on; he will also have found that workers have dropped experiments on how quickly competent adult speakers can learn or evaluate the truth or falsity of sentences of differing structure in favour of cross-cultural studies of language acquisition in infants. Such changes are not examples of planned obsolescence, but rather an almost inevitable feature of the scientific game in its early sallies into new areas, a feature to be expected rather than regretted or sneered at. It is true we do not know much about what we are talking about, but unless we make guesses and try to bring order out of ignorance, we can have no guidelines as to what to look for or where to look for it.

Not only do the latest fashions date fast, they can also be difficult to describe and discuss. In later chapters we raise questions about difficulties of successful verbal communication when speakers and listeners have different meanings paired with the same verbal units or the same meanings with different verbal units. The difficulty inheres in the venture itself: to talk or write about new problems or old problems in new ways will involve shifts in the meanings of words and disputes about this terminology.

In writing or talking about psychology and linguistics, one loses on both fronts. The 'languages' (meta-languages) in which each discipline describes and explains the phenomena within its domain of interest are both in parlous or dynamic states, pessimists preferring 'parlous' and optimists 'dynamic'. A reasonable number of problems in each are exacerbated simply because the experts cannot agree upon their terminology, although it should be remembered that the existence of different theoretical frameworks each with its own jargon is useful in so far as it keeps issues open; an agreed terminology can be an orthodoxy of ritual as well as a sign of progress made. Both disciplines, but more especially psychology, also suffer from the handicap that ordinary people have a peculiar relationship to the problems in hand, since they behave and they use language in a way in which they do not use molecules, force or DNA. This can lead to an unwarranted assumption that successful use is an index of understanding, so that people may assume that their prowess with the language means that they can talk sensibly about what language is and how it works. Unfortunately, knowing how to do something is not the same as being able to represent that knowledge symbolically; the ability to ride a bicycle can usually be more easily demonstrated than talked about in detailed terms – a specification of the sequences of neural messages required to turn a pedal being quite beyond any layman. By analogy, we can argue that detailed insight into how language functions and how we use it is not immediately available to everyone who can use it effectively. Psychology is similarly handicapped by the allegedly successful behaviour of its own subjects; people do describe and explain, control and predict the behaviour of themselves and others with a measure of efficiency, even though it is often recognized that this knowledge is not easily formulated in clear and unambiguous propositions and that what does pass for knowledge may be inadequate. Psychologists have adopted two main verbal strategies to cope with the 'knowledge' of behaviour already enshrined in our language: one is to use everyday words but to assign different meanings to them, while the second involves the creation of complete sets of neologisms. In either case would-be learners are not likely to grasp the underlying ideas quickly, but for different though equally understandable reasons. However, the difficulty is not to be avoided. In one sense it is obvious that to represent an increased understanding of behaviour will demand a new terminology. If extant systems were adequate the problems would have in all probability been solved already.

Hence we shall encounter quite a number of new words, as well as old words used in new, and hopefully more precise, senses. It may be most satisfactory to introduce these early on as far as the linguistic side of the enterprise is concerned.

What a language system is

One standard reply to questions about the nature of language is that it is a system of communication, but this will not help us far along the road; there are many systems of communication of which language is only one. Morris (1946) has argued for the usefulness of defining language as a system of communication which is composed of:

(a) a plurality of arbitrary (conventional) signs, which have
(b) a common significance to a group of organisms,
(c) a significance independent of the immediate situation, and
(d) that are produced as well as received by the users;
(e) it is a system in which the signs are articulated by certain rules of combination.

By these prescriptions Morris eliminates from consideration many communication systems often referred to as language, e.g. the language of bees, the language of the eyes (non-verbal romance) or the language of flowers (the significance of bouquets of different composition). Privately devised codes of individuals are eliminated on the criterion of common significance. There are in the man-made environment many special systems, such as road signs, which are very like languages, even to the extent of having certain limited rules of combination; but the signs are not arbitrary since features of them bear some resemblance to the phenomena depicted in a way in which the sound patterns of a language do not relate to the meanings they represent. There is also still a widespread difference in usage of the words 'signs' and 'symbols'. Here a 'sign' will be taken to be related in some non-arbitrary way to the events signified, perhaps through a causal relation or a pictorial or sonic representation. 'Symbol' will be used to refer to arbitrary relationships, or rather arbitrary relationships for which convention prescribes significance. Whichever way 'sign' and 'symbol' are contrasted, it can be argued that new or special meanings are being recommended, and this is true. It is also true that the use here is diametrically opposed to that of the translators of Piaget's work and different from Morris, but that cannot be helped. Hence for the criteria outlined by Morris, 'symbol' should be substituted for 'sign'.

Morris was not so much intending to make the language of human beings a unique accomplishment of the species as to examine the possible features that might be used to distinguish semiotic systems (semiotics being the study of sign systems), and it so happens that human language can be distinguished from systems encountered in the natural activities of other species. There have been some recent experiments intended to equip chimpanzees with a language which may bring part of the essence of this uniqueness into question. These have been founded on the premise that previous attempts (Kellog, 1968) had been unfair to chimpanzees in that they were predicated upon the anthropocentric assumption that chimpanzees should be required to learn a human language such as English – and to talk in it, in spite of their restricted articulatory capacity. Premack (1970) is attempting to teach Sarah, a chimpanzee, a non-vocal language based on combinations of pictograms (whole word units). Evidence is that Sarah is capable of trans-actions involving 8 proper names, 6 colour nouns, 21 nouns referring to foodstuffs, 25 nouns referring to other objects, 16 transitive verbs, 31 assorted adjectives, adverbs, pre-positions, and markers of such features as 'a question mark', 'not equal', 'is not', etc. Certainly Sarah's skills appear to exceed those of previous non-verbal chimpanzees, and Pre-mack's point that the 'language' should be designed to capital-ize on the learner's capacities rather than weaknesses seems obvious – in hindsight. It is noteworthy that the system being used relies on visual symbols rather than auditory ones, and that the chimpanzees appear to have needed man to inform them of their own capacities. Anyone wishing to draw parallels with early human development may also notice that obtaining foodstuffs and other desired objects figure in both situations.

Similar success is reported in the efforts of the Gardners to instruct another chimpanzee, Washoe, to use and derive new combinations of units in the American word-based sign language for the deaf and dumb (Gardner and Gardner, 1969).

More modern writers would possibly add other defining attributes of language to those of Morris. Hockett (1958), for example, mentions the seven criteria of duality, productivity, arbitrariness, interchangeability, specialization, displacement and cultural transmission. Duality refers to the coexistence of a phonological and grammatical system, pairings of significant and discriminable features with meanings. Productivity refers to the transmission of new messages, novelty of utterance. Arbitrariness refers to the relationship between the sound or writing system and the meanings of these patterns of units. Interchangeability focuses upon the abilities of speaker and listener to exchange roles, in principle at least. Specialization is more difficult to expound with its emphasis on the capacity of a signalling system to trigger off specific behaviours with precision. Messages are displaced to the extent that they are independent of the immediate physical context both in terms of what gives rise to them and what effects they have. Cultural transmission contrasts with genetic transmission as the means by which behaviours are conveyed from one generation to the next. Productivity might be extended to emphasize that the grammatical system be one which can generate, in principle, an infinite number of rule-following utterances, and it might further be required as a defining attribute that the system is capable of amendment and innovation by its users, provided a degree of consensus can be achieved.

For Chomsky, the essence of language resides in its facility for pairing patterns of sound with patterns of meaning. It should, however, be stressed that patterns are made up of units combined according to certain rules. Both *units* and *patterns* are necessary for a language system to meet Morris's criteria. One might also take issue with the stress on sound rather than sight. Linguists frequently cite the primacy of the sound system to the visually available written system, but although historically and ontogenetically this is valid, the written system has strong claims to importance in its own right in that written materials allow relatively permanent records to be made through which knowledge available can accumulate from generation to generation to an extent well beyond the capacities of an oral tradition. We have already noted that Sarah's apparent competence is not in linking sonic, but visual, symbols with meanings.

Arguments as to what is and what is not a language are certainly of interest, especially to linguists and philosophers (e.g. Hockett, 1958), but here the concern is with language in the common sense of the word, as in English, French or Urdu language, and in how it works, rather than in a subtle analysis of what it comprises.

How language works

If we restrict ourselves by way of example to languages like English and leave open the issue of whether other languages might have fundamentally different principles of organization, we are omitting both an important theoretical issue and the possibilities of demonstrating the contingency of our own system by contrast with others. People confined to a single culture often have great difficulty in conceptualizing other cultures except in terms of deviations from their own. We English speakers find it a little difficult to see that tones, clickings and even sound duration can be critical for meaning. Although this is unsurprising to some psychologists, it may nevertheless limit our capacities for seeing the characteristics of our own language system as but one of many possibilities.

Russian is not immediately comprehensible to a monolingual Englishman for several reasons. The range of sounds it uses to contrast significance are different, the rules for inflecting words (morphology) and combining them (syntax) are different, the pairing of particular sound patterns with particular grammatical words (structural vocabulary) and with lexical items (content vocabulary) is different, and the semantic categorization of the units is different (Russian and English lexical items and grammatical devices paired with each other in the dictionary are not necessarily synonymous).

The realization of these kinds of difference by English speakers has not been encouraged by an educational system which itself enshrines some odd ideas about language and how it works. The very title 'grammar' school suggests a priority for one aspect of language, and since English grammar was for many years viewed as a debased variant of Latin, which it manifestly is not, it is perhaps not surprising that we have been a little slow in enhancing our understanding. It may also be fair to add that while grammar was taught on some false assumptions, phonetics (elocution) were viewed as problems in equipping children with proper pronunciation, while increases in vocabulary size could increase the variety of items and ideas that could be referred to. Unspecified aesthetic criteria loomed large in a curriculum focused on the written rather than oral mode.

Added to this is the further limitation that children were (and are) taught to use the language rather than understand how it works. The possibility that understanding might facilitate use has hardly been explored.

Given that we can see something about the working of English by contrasting it with Russian, Latin or French, it is also true that there are similarities between Russian, English and Latin which are of an intuitively higher order than the relationship any of them bears to Chinese, Hopi, or the 'click' languages of Africa. Without an awareness of the variety of systems, it is difficult to see one's own language as enshrining but one set of choice contrasts from an infinite set. With this worry we shall proceed with English only and ask how its system works and attempt to put on two pages what no self-respecting linguist would take less than a book to describe.

We can articulate and discriminate many more sounds than our language makes use of. Babbling babies can utter an even greater variety of single sounds than adults. In English some forty-five sounds have what is called *phonemic* significance. We have these contrasting noises which can make a difference to the significance of any message we transmit – 'kit' differs from 'pit' which differs from 'git'. These units correspond only very roughly to the alphabetic writing system we utilize, which is probably one reason that people unfamiliar with the International Phonetic Alphabet (IPA) have difficulty understanding the nature of the elementary units of language. Phonemes for the most part divide into vowels and consonants; these are combined in sequences to form *morphemes*, which have meaning as well as significance. Of the three combinations of phonemes cited, 'kit' and 'pit' are different morphemes, whereas 'git' has no morphemic significance, at least in the mythical standard English. English uses only a small number of the possible combinations of phonemes to derive its morphemes, but in spite of this limitation is able to generate over 100,000 morphemes without utilizing particularly long phonemic sequences. One or more morphemes are combined to form *words* which are themselves combined into *groups*, *clauses*, and *sentences*. The rules which govern these latter four combinations constitute the grammatical system, those rules for creating words being referred to as *morphological*, those for creating groups, clauses and sentences, *syntactic*.

While already many thousands of morphemes can be made from the permitted phonemic sequences, the number of sentences that can be generated by applying the grammatical rules to appropriate units is infinite. It is these sentences we use to make our utterances and transmit our meanings. This does not imply that the sentence is the most important unit for meaning, neither are any of the others, and words as units are neither more nor less basic than phonemes. Every unit has significance at its own level of operation; while units function jointly to allow the generation of communicative utterances. The traditional focus on the word as the basic building block possibly stems from the fact that dictionaries contain words, and that words are the units bound by short silences or spaces, so possessing a superficial claim to be the most obvious units. Another reason might be that children in fact learn words as units in ways in which they do not learn phonemes, clause or sentence frames, although they do have to learn what a 'word' is.

Many of us would find it easier to write out a thousand different words than ten different sentence frames or four intonation patterns. (If the reader does not understand what that sentence means, it is presumably true.) But the situation could be otherwise. We could be taught the fundamental sentence frames or intonation patterns in the same explicit manner in which we are taught words. Words present another problem. Technically 'word' is a grammatical unit and what is called a word in everyday use would be called a *lexical item* which can and often does function as a word but may also be used in other ways. These lexical items can be divided into the two classes of *open* and *closed* sets. Of the open sets there are four in English: nouns, adjectives, verbs and adverbs. Each of these classes is characterized by having a very large membership. If we consider the sentence 'The cats are sitting on the mat', a very large number of words could be used to replace 'cats' and the grammatical acceptability of the sentence would not be affected. However, only a small number of items could substitute for 'the' or 'on'. Fries (1952) wrote about these as structural words. There are some one hundred and fifty in English, divided by Fries into fifteen classes. While it is true that many members of the form class 'noun' could substitute for 'cat', the choice of a noun as opposed to an adjective, verb, etc., is from a closed set of other *grammatical* possibilities. This range of choice is sometimes used to distinguish lexical and grammatical decisions, lexical decisions involving item selection from a large array, grammatical decisions from small ones.

The structure of the phonological and grammatical systems of English is outside our present purview. Brown (1965) gives an excellent summary for anyone whose primary interest is in psychology and child development in particular, but he does not deal extensively with semantics and not at all with pragmatics. Partly this is because we have a knowledge of phonology and grammar which can be made verbally explicit. We have labels for individual sounds (IPA); we can group them into categories using contrasts based upon manner and place of articulation. We can specify with some precision the phonological system of English in terms of articulatory and acoustic phonetics (although there remain some fascinating problems where the physical attributes of sounds fail to relate to their perceived attributes (Liberman, 1967)). We have developed many grammatical categories. While some linguists implicitly emphasize the importance of developing systems for describing instances of language by investing their energy in this direction (e.g. Halliday, 1961), others have emphasized the importance of specifying the rules by which we can most simply and elegantly generate all the grammatically acceptable sentences of a language and none of the others (e.g. Chomsky, 1965). While the descriptive linguists have not really begun to tackle semantic problems, the protagonists of generative grammar are now arguing that, at the deepest levels of analysis, a semantic theory is necessary, that there are prior problems of meaning influencing the grammatical selections and organization that will be manifested in particular utterances. Put more crudely, inaccurately and in behavioural terms, we first formulate our meanings and then organize our utterances in the light of these considerations, rather than decide to utter a passive negative question and then search for some meaning that could be expressed in this format. Unfortunately this priority accorded to semantics is currently unsupported by a strong theoretical framework, although attempts have been made (Katz and Fodor, 1963).

Earlier thoughts about *semantics* attended to relationships between the meanings of lexical items, particularly where they were readily grouped into sets and systems, e.g. kinship terms, animal terms, etc. (Brown, 1965). One can equally pose questions about the meaning of morphemes which only occur bound to other forms, e.g. the plural morpheme, or verb systems, e.g. passive. In this tradition semantics would be concerned with all contrasts of meaning at the level of each grammatical unit of analysis, rather than being a separate level in its own right. If this is so it makes sense to ask questions like which phonological distinctions have what grammatical functions with what semantic consequences. These are three different sorts of question that can be asked, all within the language system itself and in one sense independent of extra-linguistic events.

But 'semantic' has also been used to refer to the relationship of linguistic to non-linguistic events, although these concerns have been primarily a speciality of philosophers (e.g. Russell, 1912; Wittgenstein, 1951). The nature of these relationships of form to context remains uncertain. Wittgenstein wrote of the meaning of terms (and structures) being defined by their use, but others have felt there is a difficult to define but important difference between invariably successful usage and mastery of the underlying concept. Wittgenstein (1951) also wrote of propositions being 'pictures of facts', but this does not appear to be very helpful. The notion of *pragmatics* merely serves to complicate the matter further, because in this area of inquiry one is concerned to see how contextual variables are relevant to the meanings of utterances. The same utterance may convey different[1] messages according to who is saying what in what sort of atmosphere to whom, where, when, how and why – 'Ring-a-ring-a-roses a pocketful of posies' would convey different messages uttered by a teacher to five-year-old children in a games lesson, by a teacher of linguistics illustrating the achievement of poetic or rhythmic effects and by a managing director of an industrial company at a board meeting at which the members appeared to be squabbling unnecessarily. Pragmatics, as a yet nascent discipline, will focus on the manner in which contextual variables and linguistic features interact to change the significance of speech acts for a listener. To decide what an utterance is used to mean would appear then to require more information than a knowledge of the language system itself can provide.

All language functions in a context. Words exist within a linguistic context and they take significance from that context. But the utterance that provides the linguistic context, or part of it, is itself set within a context of situation and derives much of its meaning from the non-verbal elements as well as from the verbal elements present in that situation (Flower, 1966, p. 143).

1. It is to be noted that at each level of analysis mentioned the words 'contrast' and 'difference' are used with monotonous regularity, but the significance of this is often very difficult for people to grasp. The entire language system depends upon contrasts and not upon *absolute* values. In one sense everything in the system is relative.

Almost parenthetically it is worth noting that the initial attempts by psychologists to comment on the meanings of words, for example, are somewhat naïve (e.g. Brown, 1965). Linguists would quickly distinguish between linguistic and associative meaning. They would note that a word like 'table' has a linguistic meaning specifiable in semantic terms through its similarities and differences to other terms, e.g. chair, desk, dog, father; in grammatical terms through a similar set of similarities and differences; and in phonological terms also. But the word has also associative meaning, private and unique to every individual who uses it; experiences both verbal and non-verbal become attached to it – a point exploited at the verbal level by Jung most explicitly in his explorations of what came to be called word association tests. More importantly 'Such an appellative has a reservoir of flexibility and vagueness that enables us to refine its use for particular purposes',[2] e.g. water table, mathematical table, dining table, and 'under the table', 'he keeps a good table', etc. Initially perhaps through use as a metaphor in order to amuse, to be poetic, to try and point to a particular similarity or difference, to express an inchoate new idea, or to mark off social differences between groups, a word can have its meaning extended or refined and this may or may not spread through the culture.

This aspect of language, its potential for growth extending the range of meanings conveyed through the invention of new words or new uses of old ones, would appear to be a feature sadly neglected by the psycholinguists currently trapped by the perspective of transformational grammar. It is rare that any one of the entries in a dictionary has only one 'meaning' attached to it, and then of course any dictionary must inevitably fail abysmally to convey the richness of the meaning of any particular entry. The word 'table' derives its significance and meaning from the similarities and differences it has to *all* other words at all levels of analysis from the phonological through to the conceptual. To write a computer programme for a semantic memory containing even a tiny set of words is a formidable undertaking, but impressively begun by Quillian

2. I am indebted to Professor R. L. Uhlenbeck for this apt formulation.

(1966). And for this task to be extended to the 500,000 words and 300,000 technical terms offered by the *Guinness Book of Records* (McWirter and McWirter, 1970) as rough estimates of the vocabulary of the English language would tax our capacities as technological giants.

It seems that once we agree that diverse functions exist and that the meanings of particular forms are not independent of context, we are obliged to examine the functions themselves. To express relationships between meanings and forms will not tell us how particular utterances function on particular occasions, and these we must know about if we are to talk about language and social behaviour.

The division of labour

This is not intended to imply that other questions about language would not have higher priorities for persons from different disciplines. Our concern as social psychologists is not so much in how language works as a system, but how that system is used to communicate meanings to other people and what these meanings are. Just what is of interest will depend upon the discipline within which we are working. Linguists will not have exactly the same concern as social psychologists, while linguists concerned with change of usage through time in one culture (diachronic linguistics) will not necessarily collect the same set of data as linguists who are interested to examine how universal are the variants across cultures (synchronic linguistics). However, all could start with the same initial set of data collected from a single culture at a particular point in time. If we were to take (as we do in chapter 6) the case of the forms of address speakers use to call and refer to each other as an example, we could immediately pose two problems of interest to linguists and social scientists generally. What is the total range of forms available? What sociolinguistic rules govern their differential usage? Once answers to these questions have been achieved the particular perspective of the investigator will affect what other questions he will go on to ask.

In this case, a descriptive linguist might endeavour to fit his results on address forms into his general knowledge and under-standing of how the language works. He might try to write rules which would specify how address forms are fitted into the structure of sentences in grammatically acceptable ways – where they can occur in sentences and why. More generally we could say that he would wish to formulate the linguistic rules governing the integration of address forms into utterances in the language.

A sociolinguist on the other hand might ask rather different questions. What alternative forms of conveying the same message as a particular address form are available and what other message can be conveyed by alternative forms? Given the choice of a particular address form, what consequences obtain for the other elements in the utterance for it to be an internally consistent act? 'Watcha, your highness' is unlikely to occur as an utterance because it breaks rules of what goes with what. There are also rules governing the sequence of elements so that 'Jones, Christopher' will possibly mean something different from 'Christopher Jones'.

As disciplines are currently divided, the social psychologist might have interests that overlap with those of the sociolinguist, the latter creature being of such recent origin that he is as yet a hybrid rather than a pure species. The social psychologist will be interested in those contextual features of the situation which are relevant to the choice of one address form rather than another, such as the characteristics of the participants, the medium of message transmission (phone, face to face, etc.) and the situation itself (formal boardroom, informal party). He may proceed, however, to locate address forms within his understanding of non-linguistic markers of similar features and ask what non-verbal features covary with the address forms. Forms of address signal role relationships, but so do the distances chosen to separate participants, their posture, clothes, gestures and facial expressions. When address forms and other pieces of behaviour are signalling conflicting messages, which are given priority and why? In the film *The Graduate* the unenthusiastic graduate lover maintained a persistent use of 'Mrs Robinson' (no relation to the author) to his predatory mistress across the whole range of situations in which they interacted. The incongruity of the use of 'Mrs Robinson' and an intimate context deviated from social norms sufficiently to cause amusement for an audience. Just what the graduate was conveying with this address form cannot be unequivocally pinpointed. It may have been a mark of psychological if not behavioural distance, a piece of inertia in a relationship which had changed its nature very quickly, or a despairing preference for old times. These are the questions of concern to the social psychologist, but what type of rules relating language and social behaviour is he to pursue?

Sociolinguistic rules of interest to the social psychologist

Ervin-Tripp (1969) has offered a useful set of examples to illustrate three types of sociolinguistic rules: alternation, co-occurrence and sequence. 'Alternation' is a disastrous lexical choice, with its clear connotation of temporal succession. Presumably 'alternative' was the word intended, but this has no appropriate covering noun and has a semantic restriction to a binary decision, whereas the choices available may be from a wider array. In fact there would appear to be no single word in English which means 'choice of a single unit from an array of more than one'. 'Choice' itself is too general, and with some reluctance I have opted for 'substitution', while recognizing its unfortunate implication of replacement. The word 'alternative' will be used to refer to individual exponents of rules of substitution.

Rules of substititution will specify the range of choices available to an emitter at all *levels* of linguistic analysis and indicate the meanings associated with particular choices. In the extra-linguistic area we have a running 'choice' as to whether or not we include 'non-ah' speech disturbances or not. It is maintained that persons who have a relatively high incidence of such features are showing signs of anxiety (Kasl and Mahl, 1965). At the phonological level do we choose to realize 'th' as [∂] or [θ] or [d]? Members of the lower social classes in New York are more likely to be dem der dose guys (Labov, 1966). At the lexical level we can signal degrees of familiarity by choosing one form of address rather than another. Similar examples could be given for other levels of analysis.

Rules of co-occurrence have some similarity to rules of substitution but focus additionally upon the temporal extension of an utterance and whether or not each selection taken up is consistent with its both antecedent and subsequent choices (horizonal) and with the selections taken up at different levels of linguistic choice (vertical). 'I ain't bin nowhere with nobody!' may satisfy horizontal rules, but would be more likely to satisfy vertical rules if uttered in a Cockney than in an Etonian accent. In the latter case the grammatical and lexical choices might be judged odd given the phonological choices, and vice versa. Rules of co-occurrence are, as their title implies, concerned with the specification of what goes with what – and what deviation from expectation might mean.

Ervin-Tripp's third type of rule, rules of sequence, builds upon the other two by the addition of the notion of order. Given a succession of choices made in accordance with appropriate co-occurrence rules, are there set orders in which units are expected to or do occur – and what do different orders mean? Is 'Darling, hallo!' different from 'Hallo, Darling!'?

At the present time there is more interest in writing out the details of rules and rule systems (Ervin-Tripp, 1969) than in investigating why they take the form they do, especially when the rules can be got out in the format adopted by generative transformational grammar. Like transformational grammar, however, implicit presuppositions about meaning are accepted rather than discussed. In addition, the few sallies into this field have initially been within highly circumscribed areas (see chapters 6 and 7) at only certain levels of linguistic analysis, whereas in the long run all levels would have to be examined and integrated.

Ervin-Tripp's threefold division provides a useful set of questions to ask about data collected, but does not help indicate which data might be worthy of collection in the first place. Through the main chapters the notions of substitution, co-occurrence, and sequence crop up frequently if irregularly, but we need also to have some preliminary understanding of why such rules might exist.

The interaction of language and social setting

With a disarming and charming Quixotic flourish, Hymes (1967) has suggested that the term SPEAKING can itself serve as a comprehensive mnemonic to remind any investigator of the components associated with variations in speaking. They are:

(s) Setting or scene
(p) Participants or personnel
(e) Ends as (i) objectives and (ii) outcomes
(a) Art characteristics
(k) Key
(i) Instrumentalities, both (i) channel and (ii) code
(n) Norms of interaction and interpretation
(g) Genre

Not surprisingly the English language is not so accommodating to Hymes's ingenuity that he can select labels whose meanings are self-evident. 'Setting' and 'participants' are clear and appropriate. Under 'ends' are included both purpose and functions, manifest and latent: purpose referring to intentions of participants or organizers, function to what actually transpires. The two may coincide but may not. 'Art characteristics' is unfortunate, covering as it does both the 'form of a message' and its 'topic', and unintentionally but apparently relegating topic to a low level of importance. 'Key' distinguishes the tone, manner or spirit in which an act is performed, e.g. joking, solemn, gracious, etc. 'Instrumentalities' refers both to channel of transmission, itself combining speech versus writing and telephone versus face to face, while 'code' means language in the sense of Chinese versus English, with the additional rider that sub-code or variety, e.g. American English, Pakistani English, B.B.C. English, will also be a necessary further sub-division. By 'norms', Hymes intends specific rules like using an appropriate volume and not interrupting a speaker. 'Genre' classifies the type of speech act, namely, prayer, lecture, or sales talk.

These eight plus factors are offered as contextual covariants of the characteristics of verbal acts, Hymes being careful to avoid the trap of claiming that they are determinants rather than consequences. Often they will be determinants defining limits or constraints outside the speaker's control. However, the speaker has also a measure of discretion as to the values these variables may take, interacting as they do with each other as well as with the nature of verbal acts. Causal questions had best remain open until we are better informed, or until we are faced with particular empirical problems to solve; but we are probably well advised to hold a model of dynamic inter-dependence in the back of our minds rather than any unidirectional one.

The operation of these factors upon linguistic choices will be through the three types of rule enunciated by Ervin-Tripp; it is through the alternatives, co-occurrences and sequences selected that Hymes's distinctions will be realized. Hence, while Ervin-Tripp's trio points out the ways in which features of verbal behaviour can vary, Hymes is beginning to specify some of the non-linguistic variables that will be relevant to the particular selections made.

One strength of the list is that it goes beyond the linguistic notion of *register*, sometimes defined in an offhand way as 'a variety of language distinguished according to use' (Halliday, McIntosh and Strevens, 1964) where the emphasis is on variety within a language, with various scales of register offered as determinants, e.g. mode, style, participants, topic, residual. 'Mode' covers 'genre' and 'channel', 'field' is roughly equivalent to 'topic', 'style' to 'key', while 'residual' refers to the idiosyncrasies of an individual speaker. There are various definitions offered in the literature and it is not difficult to think of examples of variations in one's speech across contexts. We are, however, stuck at this stage for the present. We can offer examples of variation and can construct various categories into which these can be grouped. How to progress further is not yet clear, but at least there is a beginning. Hymes's list can be criticized adversely on many counts, but adverse evaluation without constructive alteration will not be helpful in the long run. The mnemonic has the advantage that it sensitizes the investigator to the type and range of non-linguistic factors that may be related to variations in linguistic features.

In the pursuit of a review of work relating language and social behaviour several different perspectives could be adopted. We could start with non-verbal social behaviour and steadily work through each traditional division of social psychology, showing how Ervin-Tripp's three types of rule apply in linguistic variables at each distinctive level of analysis from phonetics through to pragmatics. Hymes's categories could be used as a starting point. On the other we could start with linguistics and show how the rules of substitution, co-occurrence and sequence apply to various fields of social behaviour. Each approach would generate an ordered matrix of results readily transposed to the other. In fact neither standard procedure has been adopted, hopefully for better reasons than pure novelty.

A functional approach to language has been adopted as the organizational framework for a number of reasons, the main one being that this is not only likely to be the growth point for investigations in the next decade, but will be also the basis of the integration of linguistics and the social sciences. In so far as it is useful to envisage a contrast between social and representational uses of language, the social uses are an integral part of the study of social behaviour. The use of the clause 'I love you' can act as a substitute for a non-verbal act conveying an equivalent message; it may only convey this message if uttered in a context where many other variables are set at appropriate values. When particular verbal acts function as equivalents of non-verbal ones and when their occurrences are necessary or sufficient conditions of the communication of certain messages, are matters for empirical investigation. What linguistic structures can be used or are used may be better treated as a secondary problem. Of course it would be as absurd to neglect structures at the expense of functions as it would to neglect functions at the expense of studying structures. Always both have to be kept in mind. My personal judgement is that linguistics itself has been unduly weighted with structural analyses in both the Bloomfieldian and post-Bloomfieldian eras. This is not to decry the usefulness of such enterprises, although my personal and tentative suspicion is that they are based on a fundamental error of judgement as to how language works.

The case for a concentration upon functions, with subsequent illustrative rather than comprehensive reviews of other linguistic and non-linguistic features associated with these, is argued more fully in chapter 2.

2 Functions of Language

Reasons for a functional/structural approach

If we ask why the study of the functions of language has not been treated as a basic set of problems, we are posing a question to which no clear cut answers can be given, but at least some guesses might be made.

In the first place 'functional' models are currently unpopular in both the physical and biological sciences – and for good reasons. They sometimes have teleological overtones and leave unanswered many other questions associated with the phenomena observed. Questions like 'What are electrons for?' would probably be ruled as inappropriate in the discourse of electronics. Even if we were to allow electrons an existential rather than a conceptual status, we would not consider answers like 'To carry negative electric charges' as good physics. We may ask what characteristics electrons display and how they relate to other atomic or sub-atomic particles, but they are not *for* anything, they just are – or we might prefer to say that the concept of 'electron' is useful. In zoology, to ask why whales have 'fins' is more likely to be answered in terms of development from evolutionary ancestors than 'In order to swim'. However, the zoologist might well be interested in the functions of fins and how fins serve these, but as part of a total network of interest rather than the central core of his explanatory story. In its early days the behavioural science of psychology was so concerned with its status as a science that physics was often held up as an ideal to which psychology aspired, and the notion of what a good theory should be was influenced in much the same way as the methodology: hypothetico-deductive theories with clearly derivable and experimentally testable predictions were the dream. By the 1930s it was permissible but not entirely respectable to think in terms of means-ends relationships; Tolman's description and explanation of rat behaviour leaned heavily on purposive notions of goals 'pulling' animals towards them, but it is perhaps nonetheless significant that Hull's 'pushing' causal model has been a more influential background for subsequent research. The functional-causal dichotomy is one of those dilemmas on whose horns it is in fact unnecessary to impale oneself, stemming as it does from what are currently labelled 'convergent' ways of thinking about a problem which has no unique solution. The dichotomy presupposes that there is a best type of explanation and that there is *one* best that we are seeking. Once we can see that different types of explanation provide understanding of different aspects of the same phenomenon, and that *all* are of interest if they correspond with reasonable constructions of reality, we have escaped from the one-answer-only mentality. While functional explanations in biological sciences are only one type of explanation and run the risk of being quickly circular, the posing of functional questions can often be a useful framework from which to pursue inquiry. For example, asking why embryonic chicks should have gills may provoke thinking along fruitful lines.

However, functional analyses may have an even stronger claim to importance once the interest is in systems or devices created by man. It is not odd to ask what chairs or cars are for in the same way that it is odd to ask what wood or tigers are for. The one set of objects has reasons for existence only because some function is or was served by them. It is possible for new functions to be found for systems invented for different purposes, but if we adopt a simple-minded or child-like approach it is far from absurd to ask what man-made systems are or were for.

Language is a man-made system. We may not find it useful to attempt to discern what functions it originally served and we may not immediately wish to ask what new functions it can be used to serve, but to ignore the functions of what is essentially a technological innovation would seem to be a very odd policy.

Such a prescription does not relegate problems of the structure of language to an insignificant role, but does imply that purely structural analyses will be only partially informative. At some stage it is necessary to examine the relationships between functions and structures.

We have referred to functions as plural because we would be rash in presupposing that there is one single function when a cursory consideration suggests more than one. Given that this is so, we shall have to generate a list or lists of different functions. Any such list may eventually contain several independent functions or we may find that we can usefully group certain of them together, but in either case some classification will be necessary. This may be another reason why such an approach has been avoided. Listing has not been popular in psychology in recent years. At one time, lists of the different human instincts (McDougall, 1908), needs (Murray, 1938) or traits (Cattell, 1957) were generated – and promptly criticized on the grounds that they were arbitrary and lacking the operationally defined measurement that would reveal the utility of the separations made. In the field of human motivation, interest switched from content and classification to process and explanation of how 'motives' interacted with other factors to produce behaviours of certain types and vigour (see Atkinson, 1964). There was of course a necessary tacit assumption that the drives so investigated had some justification for their isolation. Similarly, in the investigations of the relationships between generative grammar and behaviour, the concern has been focused on a study of processes for a limited set of transformations (e.g. the development, encoding or decoding of passive, negative or interrogative sentences) rather than upon a listing of transformations actual or possible. One suspects too that theories of how processes work accrue greater distinction to their authors than do taxonomies of content, and additionally evoke more interest from research workers. It is perhaps also more enjoyable to test predictions from a theory than to probe into the utility of a classificatory system, which in itself cannot be used to generate testable hypotheses at all.

A third reason for the neglect of functions may be found in

the current state of linguistics. Phonetics, phonology, grammar, lexicography all have an accumulated wisdom. Whole books can be written on each one, workers have frameworks within which to operate or against which to rebel or revolt. Semantics and pragmatics do not have this background to anywhere near the same extent. It is a little safer to sail in the seas which have navigational charts, than to wallow about in a mass of water.

It could be argued that although linguists have not yet thrown their intellects at problems of semantics and pragmatics, philosophers have been doing so for a long time, so many of them that it would be absurd to cite references. Perhaps a would-be sailor should read such charts as philosophers have produced about meaning in language before embarking upon his own voyage. A daunting prospect if ever there was one.

A final reason may be sought in a misunderstanding of the nature of a language system itself. Just as within any analysis of the structure of the grammatical system we cannot use a single fundamental concept like 'word' or 'sentence' but must use both, so any analysis of the total system and how it works must relate structure and function. Structures, being arbitrary, can only derive their significance in function. This is not to say that the two are inextricably interlocked so that a conceptual distinction between them cannot be made, but simply that any utterance qualifying as a communicative act will have both a structure and function. Structural analyses have never in fact eliminated notions of meaning and function, but the emphasis on structure has often been so strong as to lead the unwary into an impression that function is irrelevant. If we are to succeed in the enterprise of understanding how language works in practice, we shall have to show how these two interrelate – and that will mean an analysis of functions as well as structures.

Given that these points have some force, it is perhaps not surprising that psychologists interested in how people use language should shy away from a functional approach: the historical tradition of psychology with its limited conception of the nature of inquiry, the strength of linguistics in phonology and grammar, as well as wishes for fame and fun, severally militate against such an endeavour.

Since the development of a list of functions of language is not among the highest priorities of workers in the language field, any list offered at this stage is likely to be arbitrary and amenable to only weak forms of defence in that, while it cannot be shown to be wrong with a quick brilliant experiment, such investigations cannot immediately help to support it either.

Classifications of functions

There are lists extant and it may be worthwhile to examine some of these, since they may open up some of the problems of classification. Social psychologists have long been concerned with a topic referred to generally as *content analysis* (e.g. Pool, 1959; Holsti, 1968). This has involved the development of categories which it is hoped will capture behaviourally relevant features of samples of language. Content analysis has been used heavily in relation to the outpourings of the mass-media. We may wish to compare the dominant concerns of different daily newspapers or the different positions adopted by them towards particular issues. We may wish to see how content changes through time. People have plotted the contents of such papers as *Isvestia* and *Pravda* through time as being indicative of Soviet friendliness or hostility to the United States or China (Berelson, 1952). The technique may rely on simple assumptions that the amount of space devoted to a topic is related to the salience of it, or that overt statements of hostility reflect hostile attitudes. As far as language use is concerned, attitudes are inferred from verbal statements proffered. A wide variety of measures of behaviour from natural observation of behaviour, through questionnaires to clinically used projective tests, such as the Rorschach or Thematic Apperception Test, can rely on an analysis of the content of speech given as a basis for inference. It is not always assumed that a high rate of mentioning a topic goes with salience, the reverse might hold in some clinical settings; it is not always assumed that statements of friendliness are sincere, but rules have been devised and evidence collected to help decide what is to count as having what meaning (e.g. Atkinson, 1958). Content analysis is normally exploited to find out what the emitter is thinking or feeling rather than what functions the verbal behaviour is performing, and the classificatory systems utilized are usually intended to elicit information about the types and strengths of motives, values or attitudes rather than a specification of other information that might be transmitted.

This is not so much the case with the analyses made of the behaviour of small groups, especially those which are given a specific problem to solve, such as reaching a jury-type of decision on an accused or obtaining the answer to a mathematical puzzle. Although several general systems for classifying behaviour in small groups have been devised which may make use of anything from four to ninety-six categories (Carter, Haythorn, Meirowitz and Lanzetta, 1951), it is probably most sensible to describe briefly the one most frequently used, namely Bales's *Interaction Process Analysis* (1950).

This system was devised to facilitate the description of how problem-solving groups work; how roles differentiate, how norms are formed and enforced, how sentiments develop. In its most commonly used version, the system has twelve categories (see Figure 1).

Each category has its complementary, six with features purported to move the group towards success and six which do not, while four are concerned with internal relational problems and eight with task analysis and solution. Although observers are required to record the non-verbal as well as the verbal acts, the groups typically studied have been of such a character that most raw data have been based on verbal acts. It therefore represents a classification of verbal acts in terms of what people are doing when they use language. Bales (1950) produced a manual giving definitions of his categories and instructions for scoring, and people can be trained relatively quickly to agree on the categorization of the units of analysis. The utility of the system is attested, incidentally by the number of research workers who have chosen to employ it, but mainly through its pre-eminence in work leading to the empirical and theoretical advances in our understanding of the behaviour of problem-solving groups (Cartwright and Zander, 1960; Golembiewski, 1962). The application of the system is narrow in scope, but within these limits,

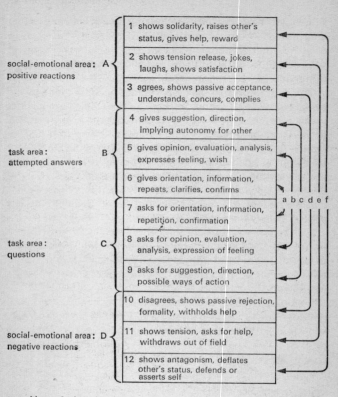

social-emotional area: A
positive reactions

1 shows solidarity, raises other's status, gives help, reward

2 shows tension release, jokes, laughs, shows satisfaction

3 agrees, shows passive acceptance, understands, concurs, complies

task area: B
attempted answers

4 gives suggestion, direction, implying autonomy for other

5 gives opinion, evaluation, analysis, expresses feeling, wish

6 gives orientation, information, repeats, clarifies, confirms

task area: C
questions

7 asks for orientation, information, repetition, confirmation

8 asks for opinion, evaluation, analysis, expression of feeling

9 asks for suggestion, direction, possible ways of action

social-emotional area: D
negative reactions

10 disagrees, shows passive rejection, formality, withholds help

11 shows tension, asks for help, withdraws out of field

12 shows antagonism, deflates other's status, defends or asserts self

a b c d e f

a problems of orientation
b problems of evaluation
c problems of control
d problems of decision
e problems of tension management
f problems of integration

Figure 1 Interaction process analysis coding categories

it sets a precedent for the potential of a functional approach to language usage.

Ervin-Tripp (1964) used a different set of categories for describing the initiation of two-person interactions: requests for goods, services, information, requests for social responses, offering information or interpretation, expressive monologues, routines (greetings, apologies, etc.), avoidance conversations (talking where not talking would be more unpleasant). While this list may have been useful for the purposes of the investigation, it appears to lack the orderliness and completeness of Bales's system which makes explicit the similarities and differences between categories. But then the categories have yet to be refined by a large number of subsequent investigations.

These two examples from social psychology may be contrasted with three proposed by linguists. Firth (cited in Hymes, 1964) offered a classification based primarily on the social value of speech acts: phatic communion (attainment and maintenance of group solidarity), pragmatic efficiency (accompanying work), planning and guidance, address (greetings, farewells, adjustment of relations), and speech as commitment (courts, promises).

More recently, Halliday posed the problem from an educational point of view proposing that:

We shall try to identify the models of language with which the normal child is endowed by the time he comes to school at the age of five, the assumption being that if the teacher's own 'received' conception of language is in some way less rich or less diversified, it will be irrelevant to the educational task (1969, p. 28).

He then examined six models of language that might be imputed to or inferred from the behaviour of a five-year-old child: instrumental, regulatory, interactional, personal, heuristic and imaginative.

In a concluding statement at a symposium, *Style in Language*, Jakobson (1960) (see Figure 2) offered an artistically presented classification linking functions with different possible prime foci of an utterance. He took six aspects of the speech event – addresser, addressee, context, message, contact and code – and associated a focus on each of these with functions labelled respectively: emotive (expressional), conative, referential, poetic, phatic and metalingual. Illustrating each with examples, Jakobson achieved a measure of systematization in that we can see how by shifting the point of interest we change the sorts of question that we can pose about an utterance. Neat, but relatively undeveloped and incomplete, except with respect to the poetic function, which was after all Jakobson's immediate interest.

Figure 2 Functions of language distinguished by focus of attention (after Jakobson, 1960). Capital letters are used to denote the object of focus, italics for functions

These 'models' indeed embrace a wide range of activities, much wider than those included under the two examples from social psychology, but their definitions are far from precise and they are given no structural realizations nor possible differentiating concomitants on the behavioural side. No evidence is given in support of this type of division rather than any other, with a final worry lying, for example, in Halliday's comment that his categories are not independent of each other, although he does not proceed to add in what ways they are not.

These criticisms are set down to indicate the sort of questions that would have to be asked eventually about any fully-fledged taxonomy, rather than to suggest that Halliday's proposals, for example, are not worthy of consideration. When ignorance and chaos abound, the first step is to impose some order rather than hope for an immediate final solution.

A comparison of the lists from social psychology and linguistics does yield some requirements that a final taxonomy of functions of language should meet:

1. It should cover all uses of language. That the system should be hierarchical as well as categorical is apparent from the Bales's analysis in which categories can readily be grouped together to form higher order units like 'analysing problem', 'synthesizing solution' or 'problem-solving'. In this respect it would be similar to classificatory systems in botany, zoology or chemistry – or even grammar. It is also virtually certain that no hierarchy could be represented in two-dimensional space. We can quickly see that 'offering information' could occur both in the analysis of a problem and the synthesis of its solution.

2. As an insurance policy against a possible failure to be exhaustive and because social psychologists would also be interested in them, a classification of functions might well include paralinguistic and extralinguistic features of utterances. That they might be treated separately later is true, but in the early stages of an attempt to be comprehensive it is better to make the frame of reference too wide rather than too narrow.

3. Such categories as are used should be clearly definable:
(i) For Aristotle, a good definition of a term in a system was one that specified its relationship to all other terms in that system, especially in so far as similarities and differences were concerned.
(ii) Verbal definition is essential, but needs to be supplemented by indications of how the category is to be reliably recognized when it occurs. In principle at least the category must be capable of operational definition, wherever possible in terms of

the linguistic forms unique or possible within that function. When this cannot be achieved, contextual information relevant to identification should be given. The greater the extent to which these definitions can be linked to concepts already available in linguistics, psychology and other behavioural sciences, the better.

4. It should be realized that any taxonomy will be inadequate. The inadequacy stems partly from the nature of language itself, and partly from human behaviour. Both have possibilities for change and re-organization within and beyond our present imaginings. The inadequacy also stems from the degree of generality attempted. To have any generality entails missing some contrasts that could be made. For particular and limited objectives more detailed analysis of the situations under consideration will be required, but it is hoped that the general framework can keep investigators sensitive to functions over and above those hopefully contained within their immediate perspective.

As often happens, when the general and abstract problems remain intractable, research workers can be faced with practical problems of coding data in particular limited settings and these can throw light upon future developments. Soskin and John (1963) had to devise a scoring system for varied verbal ways of achieving an objective – in this case, borrowing a coat. They derived six categories:

1. 'It's cold today.' (structone)
2. 'Lend me your coat.' (regnone)
3. 'I'm cold.' (signone)
4. 'That looks like a warm coat you have.' (metrone)
5. 'Brrh.' (expressive)
6. 'I wonder if I brought a coat.' (excogitative)

These categories are based on function, but have linguistically different realizations, for example 'excogitative' always expresses uncertainty utilizing excogitative lexical items. A case could be argued for the regnone being primitive – in this example it is the only explicit attempt to claim the coat –

and the others derived or secondary; but when and where each in fact occurs with what frequency as context, participants, type of transaction and medium of communication vary poses empirical questions. In this case Dikeman and Parker (see Ervin-Tripp, 1969) have used the system to examine what goes on in a small sample of American families. They found that indirect request forms were more common than regnones among persons of equal status, but were less common than regnones when persons of lower status addressed those of higher status, and that the two were roughly equal in occurrence when higher status persons addressed lower status persons. In occupational settings however, high status persons when addressing sub-ordinate lower status persons were more likely to use regnones.

With such a system as a starting point we may examine in the first place how settings and relationships affect the pattern of the form requests take. By linking the results found with beliefs we may have (or can extract from participants) about the differential meaning of the different forms of request (e.g. politeness, etc.), we can devise test situations which will probe the validity of our interpretations. As our knowledge of the relevant determinants of choice expands, we can attempt to integrate types of interaction, other than requests into the system, and so on.

The Soskin and John approach exemplifies one strategy and within its pretended scope appears to be successful. Not only are the categories understandably defined in linguistic terms, their utilization in empirical settings has begun to show up differences in behaviour of relevance to social psychology.

A taxonomy of functions

Unfortunately the present frame of reference requires the pro-duction of a more comprehensive scheme set out in Table 1. It is represented as an extension of Jakobson's version in Figure 3. A number of categories are taken from taxonomies already referred to, while others have been invented. The scheme is by no means complete, and probably not exhaustive. The func-tions are not all at the same level of analysis, certain types of role relationship for example being marked by differential

Table 1 Functions of language

Function	Everyday name of activity or products	Prime focus of verbal act	'Primitive' linguistic forms General	Examples	Basis of Evaluation
1. Avoidance worse activity	Escapism (verbal)	Participants	Any within constraints of context		Saved from other problems?
2. Conformity to norms	Speech and writing	Rule subscription	Any within constraints of context		Did you keep going without awkward silences? Did the corpus appear to be a speech, essay, etc.?
3. Aesthetics	Literature, poetry, drama, novel, rhetoric	Message form	Often well defined, but above rank of sentence. Beyond micro-linguistics	Sonnets; tragedies; fables	Beautiful, insightful, moving?
4. Encounter regulation	Greeting, leave taking	Participant interaction	A finite set of special words, noises, and phrases. Pausing, questions	Hi! Jane! Chow! What do you think?	Attention attracted? Contact made? Flow maintained? Ending satisfactory?
5. Performatives	Promising, betting, etc.	Non-verbal accomplishments	A finite set of semantically associated verbs used in normatively and legally prescribed forms	I name this ship the *Bubbly Bosun*	Intended act performed?
6. Regulation of self (i) behaviour (ii) affect	Talking to oneself, prayer, etc.	Emitter	Abbreviated imperatives?	Now, one teaspoon mustard, Pull yourself together	Is performance in fact facilitated by talking? Is affective state changed or induced?
7. Regulation of others (i) behaviour (ii) affect	Commands, requests, threats, jibes, jokes	Receiver	Imperatives, closed questions, model verbs, etc. A finite set of semantically associated verbs and phrases. Set forms of humour	Jump! Will you . . .? You must . . . If . . . then . . . You creep. Puns; sick jokes	Obedience obtained? Dissuaded? Humiliated? Made to laugh?

8. Expression of affect	Exclamations, swearing	Emitter	Vocatives, swear words, terms of endearment	Oh my love! × × × ×!	Do you feel better?
9. Marking of emitter (i) emotional state (ii) personality (iii) identity	— — —	Emitter	Para- and extra-linguistic features; overt statements. Phonology (accent) grammatical, lexical choices	I, I, I think… I'm scared. 'otel; ain't no … lavatory	Correct diagnosis made or impression conveyed?
10. Role relationship marking	—	Relationship emitter receiver	Rights and duties to use of socially prescribed forms of address, and forms of utterance	Sir! Sweetie! Let us pray	Choice and sequence right for accepted ways of defining roles?
11. Reference to non-linguistic world involving: discrimination, organization, storage, transmission, instruction in spheres of knowledge: (i) logics, (ii) science (iii) ethics, (iv) metaphysics, (v) aesthetics	Many: stating, arguing, reporting, remembering, thinking(?), problem-solving, analysing, processing, synthesizing	Correspondence of verbal act to non-verbal world	Declarative sentence forms	The cat is on the mat. If A, then B! Doggie will bite! All gone, daddy	True or false within premisses of universe of discourse? Is argument valid? Are rules of game followed?
12. Instruction	Teaching	Acquisition new skills by receiver	Various		Did you learn?
13. Inquiry	Questioning	Acquisition knowledge for emitter	Interrogative form	What is he on about?	Does it serve to fill the appropriate gap in your knowledge?
14. Meta-language functions	—	—	—	—	—

rights to control the behaviour of others, combining two functions. It makes naïve assumptions about relationships between form and function.

The first column lists functions, while the second notes words or phrases commonly used to refer to the relevant activity, should it have a name. The third attempts to apply Jakobson's notion of focus of the verbal event, while the fourth and fifth mention linguistic features which may be peculiarly or commonly associated with a given function. The final column mentions questions which may be asked to determine whether or not the verbal act was successful. This last is probably the most useful feature of the table, because the constituent questions exemplify the empirical testing procedure against which the significance of any verbal event can be tested. It cannot be assumed very simply that a speaker can be asked whether or not what he was saying was true or simply filling up time or a leg-pull. His overt reason may well differ from his real reason; his purpose may not correspond to the function; he will not even be aware of the underlying reasons for making Freudian slips – if Freud's interpretation of such events is correct. Hence there is no implication that the diagnosis of function is a simple and certain matter, but the elaboration of a technology of diagnosis would seem to be the focal point for the growth of our understanding of how language works in context.

There are certain possibilities of misunderstanding about the proposed list of functions that need to be dispelled. Firstly, any verbal event may simultaneously serve several functions. 'I bet you £5!' may well be said in a context where it marks features of state, personality and identity, constitutes an attempt to control another's behaviour and, if accepted, is a performative utterance. A multi-functional analysis of a verbal event will be the rule rather than the exception – and perhaps a universal rule.

Secondly, many of the functions can be performed without reliance upon language. Not only do the para- and extra-linguistic features of a verbal act serve functions shared by the linguistic features, non-verbal alternatives may act as substitutes. The outstretched arm of a stern looking father pointing at the stairs can substitute for 'It's time you went to bed.'

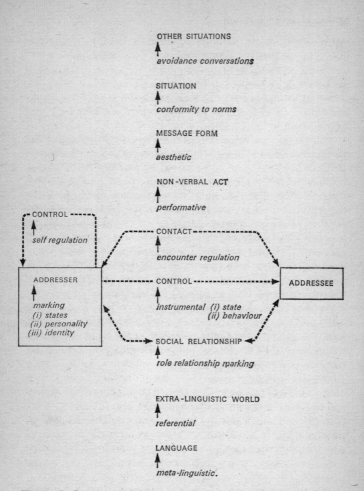

Figure 3 Functions of language. Capital letters mark the focus, italics are used for functions

Music may evoke emotional responses similar to those produced in a hearer through the aesthetic use of language.

On the other hand, other communicative acts may be either very difficult or impossible to perform without a reliance upon a use of language. This will be particularly relevant in the referential use of language for many topics, e.g. history, social administration, law, chemistry, etc.

Thirdly, the use of certain features or structures will not of themselves lead to 'successful' communicative acts. As Austin (1962) points out with his analyses of naming ships, a large number of other necessary conditions must be met for the utterance 'I name this ship the *Mary Jane*!' to be happy, as he terms it: the speaker must be the duly authorized person in the right place at the proper time swinging the traditional bottle of shortly-to-be-wasted champagne. In a two-person encounter a speaker's announcement that he is sorry that he, rather than the other person, was offered the job for which they both applied may be judged 'insincere', if the para- and extra-linguistic features of the utterance are not those customarily associated with regret, e.g. if the speaker's face has a broad smile and he is jumping with joy. In such a situation there are many variables of distance, posture, gesture and expression that must *all* take on consonant values for the manifest content of the verbal utterance to be judged credible. (This particular problem is expanded upon in chapter 6.)

The column headed 'primitive' linguistic features and/or forms heads a list of weak definitions that would make a linguist flush – with embarrassment or anger. As the examples of Soskin and John (see p. 48) show, there are many ways in which an utterance may serve as an attempt to borrow a coat.

It was suggested that only the regnone 'Lend me your coat!' makes the speaker's request explicit, while conventions of politeness and role relationships will dictate the detailed form that this might take (presumably 'I wonder if I might borrow that coat' is a deferentially polite form of regnone rather than an excogitative). The others could be referential comments on the weather (structone), one's own body temperature (signone), or the listener's good fortune (metrone). The excogitative 'I wonder if I brought a coat' is a heuristic utterance concerned with matters of reference, while 'Brrh!' is a simple expressive. We would normally refer to these as veiled hints, although it must be conceded that the cultural conventions might be quite unambiguous. A slightly embarrassing cross-cultural difficulty arises when British people pass favourable comments on the possessions of Russians, Arabs and others. What was intended to be a friendly appreciation of a piece of jewellery and a compliment to a host is liable to result in an insistent demand that you accept it as a gift.

In what sense can the notion of 'primitive' be defended? Certainly no claim to historical precedence is being made. Neither is there an implication that the individual child will learn primitive forms first and others later. There might be a defence in terms of a consensus of what the fictitious normal adult speaker of a language would say about 'sentences': imperatives are used for giving orders, declaratives are used for making statements which have a truth value, given certain premises, and vocatives are used for making expressive utterances. For encounter regulation and the marking of states, personality and identity, and role definition, we can appeal to the evidence accumulated and reviewed in subsequent chapters. We may note that, as with certain other social facts, the diffusion of knowledge concerning their operation may well lead to changes in their operation. When people become aware of how the use of non-U words can identify their social status, they may change their choices. As Labov (1966) has demonstrated, lower middle class New Yorkers are prone to overcorrect their pronunciation of some phonemes in formal settings. Similarly one might expect that persons anxious to conceal their anxiety may learn enough about signs of this state to correct their performance. We all encounter situations in which we are tempted to perform rather than be ourselves, and the more we know about the criterial attributes of our intended mask, the greater the chances of wearing it convincingly. However, although the particular values taken by variables may change in their actual significance, the differentiations achieved are likely to remain. In the area of role relationships of superior–

inferior, the linguistic features used to differentiate in Standard Average European titles and pronouns of address have changed through time, and changed differently in different cultures; the means of differentiation abide, although a non-reciprocal use of *tu* and *vous* may no longer mark it.

However, the contemporary *status quo* constitutes the baseline from which shifts occur, and in this sense this basis and its traceable history are primitive linguistic features. In this case primitive is a relational rather than a categorical term, serving to contrast elaborations and alterations from previous states.

With these provisos, the scheme is offered as a classificatory system against which the possible significance of particular verbal events can be evaluated. Those functions of especial interest to social psychologists interested in language are discussed in separate chapters, while those of less immediate concern are grouped and relegated to a single chapter.

3 Functions of Language Described

The extent to which comment can be made about functions as set out here differs with the present state of the art: some functions have not been thought about or investigated at all, others have been thought about, while yet others have been investigated. The extent of comment is restricted also by the consideration of relevance. Those functions which have both direct relevance to social psychology and have been investigated from that perspective are treated cursorily in this chapter, but in detail later. Those functions either uninvestigated or of lesser immediate relevance to social psychology are treated in more detail, but not mentioned thereafter. With a touch of perversity the order of treatment relegates what many people would regard as the unique and major functions of language to the end of the chapter. Hopefully this will cause people to hesitate a little and ask whether or not they are focusing upon a topic or only conforming to norms.

It would be a strange variety of social psychologist who suggested that 'conformity to norms' was not relevant to his discipline; but this function, along with 'avoidance of other problems', is treated cursorily here because the linguistic features themselves which are associated with them are to a considerable extent irrelevant to the main concern, *viz.* how specific features of language work in specific situations.

Verbal behaviour as a means of avoiding other problems

It is alleged that some teenagers, and some not-so-teenagers, plug themselves into continuous transistorized music to save themselves from thinking. This allegation can be supported superficially by casual interviewing and, although not yet systematically investigated, it seems evident that self-selected exposure to patterned sequences of stimulation of various sorts can be used to delay or avoid dealing with problems. Talking to oneself, writing, and conversation with other people are among such devices, along with drugs, alcohol, watching television or playing bridge. A virgin field of study and likely to be a fertile one in so far as the incidence of such activities may well be high in contemporary industrialized societies.

From the point of the social psychologist interested in language, however, it may not matter much what is said or how it is said, if the primary purpose and functioning of the speaking is simply to distract attention from other thoughts. It is unlikely that particular features of language will be linked to this function, although one might expect utterances to be fairly heavily sprinkled with well-rehearsed phrases of a ritualistic nature. The field is perhaps most likely to be ploughed first by clinical psychologists, who are unlikely to assume that speech directed to this end will be random. Speaking to no ordinary purpose could be construed as an extreme type of projective test, and hence its structure and content might be amenable to constructive examination.

It should not be difficult to distinguish between compulsive talking and filibustering, where the reasons for attempting to achieve delays should be more readily discernible.

Conformity to norms

'There is a time to speak and a time to keep silence.' The rules governing the occasions for silence and speech differ from culture to culture, but all cultures will have such rules. In our society these norms will differ from group to group and from situation to situation. Quaker meetings for worship can enjoy an hour's silence; the House of Commons commonly does not. Railway carriages in the south of England have a reputation for respecting privacy; silences of short duration at parties represent failure. Radio stations apparently have to confine their periods of silence to seconds rather than minutes to avoid questioning phone calls.

It is easy to conceive of situations where the person who can talk is at a premium: post-funeral breakfasts, meetings of strangers, reunion dinners, hospital visiting, and so on. It can be a relief to have someone present who will keep talking regardless of topic, interest or even propriety. But these settings are not the only ones where sustained verbal activity is required. When was a newspaper last published with a column blank except for a notice announcing that there was insufficient news to fill the space that day? How often does an 'expert' interviewed on television or radio admit that he has nothing to say in reply to a question posed? As a personal and inadequate investigation it is masochistically instructive to be honest and say, 'I'm too ignorant of the facts to venture an opinion' in reply to requests for views about international events. Our norms appear to dictate that an opinion be offered in reply to a request for one, and to admit that one's knowledge is inadequate may be as socially maladroit as to inquire too deeply into the evidence underpinning the opinions of others. Breaking conventions is often an illuminating way of testing their force.

We can go a little further and ask how often pupils in any educational organization admit they do not understand or even know when they do not? How often, on the other hand, do they feel constrained to offer some answer, perhaps successfully 'psyching' out (another American contribution to the English language) the teacher and saying or writing what he approves of? Informed pessimists might argue that this is the commonest influence on pupils' products, that a student's main problem is to evoke certain responses from teachers or peers and that understanding the subject matter has a low place in the scale of priorities. For example, a university student submitting an essay could have a hierarchy of priorities. The essay must cover four foolscap sides; the writing should be almost legible; the prose should be in reasonably acceptable English; it should cite references; it should be sprinkled with the appropriate jargon – and it must be done by Thursday. The logical structure of the arguments may have less importance, and that what is written should have a correspondence to a construction of reality relevant to the topic (referential function) almost none.

It might be thought that problems of conformity to norms are indistinguishable from matters of signalling role relationships. The first examples given might be viewed as situations in which someone is obliged to take on the role of speaker and others listeners, while the tutorial essay is a product of and marks the pupil–teacher role relationship. In a general sense this is so, but more specifically a contrast can be drawn between situations which demand some verbalization and those which focus on the social relationship between participants. In the former, issues of superiority/inferiority or familiarity are secondary: students will not normally be penalized if they re-order their priorities and show care about the relationships between what they write and the topic they are writing about. By contrast, a teacher who is obsessively concerned to assert power over pupils might actually require them to write un-truths, thereby indicating who is boss. Although these two functions are related, it should be possible to differentiate be-tween them by examining where the priorities lie and which changes in the verbal events are acceptable and which not. In the case of the essay, and in many others, additional informa-tion would be required to answer the question, since identical pieces of work could derive from at least two different sources of influence.

As with 'avoidance of other problems', speech or writing functioning to conform to norms will be diverse in form, and possibly punctuated with a similar sprinkling of well-rehearsed sequences. Where the intention is to pass comment on the real world, we may expect a number of distinguishing features. If the referential use were genuine, there should be a corres-pondence between what is said and the extralinguistic world, or at least signs of a concern about such a correspondence. We might expect distinctions drawn between what is known and what is not known, what is known and what is believed. There should be a concern that arguments are logically consistent and that appropriate evidence can be marshalled in support of statements offered. When these conditions do not apply, when some of the thirty-two ways of cheating in arguments outlined by Thouless (1953) occur, and their exposure is greeted with another of them rather than with gratitude, conformity to norms is a candidate for consideration.

In the field of social behaviour, conformity at the level of verbal utterance was a lively area of investigation before Sherif's (1936) and Asch's (1952) demonstrations of the effect of group norms upon verbal reports. Social desirability of answers has been a nagging methodological headache in questionnaire design (Edwards, 1957; Scott, 1968) and by implication in everyday behaviour as well, as can be seen in studies of inter-racial and political verbal and non-verbal, and public and private verbal behaviour. If Kohlberg's (1969) initial results are replicated, the dominant mode of adult thinking about moral problems in contemporary America, at least as inferred from verbal reports, is based upon conformity; in men, conformity to notions of preserving law and order, and in women, conformity to the opinions of significant other individuals in their immediate environment.

Comment

Although for neither 'avoidance of other problems' nor 'conformity to norms' are there clearly definable and simple investigations of direct appeal to social psychologists whose dominant concern is in the use of language, there are many possibilities for exploratory work in this area. Language used for these functions appears to be a dependent variable, but how far this is so, and whether it might also function as an independent variable maintaining a *status quo*, we do not know; but one way in which this might be so is illustrated in chapter 9, where special attention is paid to the social class differences in the use of language in socialization.

Aesthetics

To relegate the aesthetic functions of language to a paragraph or two borders on philistinism. In ordinary conversation we may try to express ourselves beautifully, at dinners and cocktail parties even more so, revelling in witty turns of phrases, especially when we create our replies retrospectively! In poetry, plays, rhetoric and novels the aesthetic criteria loom even larger. Linguistic constraints abound, but refer mainly to units above the rank of sentence and hence beyond the present reach of contemporary mainstream linguistics. Certain forms of poems have special names: epics, ballads and sonnets. These forms may prescribe the number of lines in a poem, the length and metrical characteristics of each line, and rhyming patterns. Sonnets have fourteen lines, divided into a set of eight (octave) and six (sestet), the break often marking a semantic shift. The lines are of ten syllables, the metre iambic (short-long). Three different schemes of rhyme yield the Petrarchan, Shakespearean and Miltonic variants. The sonnet has a particularly detailed specification, but similar considerations apply to other types of poem.

With these constraints that do not apply to everyday conversation go certain freedoms. Grammatical rules can be waived or rare forms employed in the interests of the poet's objectives. Artists in the service of their muse are officially accorded poetic licence which allows normally referential constraints to be made subservient. Time and space may be abused, objects may acquire impossible attributes – 'Nature might stand up to all the world and say, *This was a man*!' – a most unlikely contingency and what a reconstruction of the universe to achieve a rather obvious utterance. But then we do not ask whether or not statements in poetry are literally true. We ask whether they are insightful or moving, whether they express 'deep truths' not readily conveyed in referential statements anchored in reality, and whether they are beautiful.

Similarly with other art forms possessing a wholly or heavy verbal component, there are special systems and conventions, and the criteria of evaluation are not those we apply to scientific or everyday statements. It can be maintained that this is necessarily so, that poetry would have no *raison d'être* if its messages could be conveyed within the framework of rules governing everyday speech.

Since the aesthetic function will regretfully not be mentioned again, we might note here certain problems that its existence poses for the developing child. If language may be thought of as the raw material of a game, then poetry is a meta-game, i.e. a game within or on top of a game. The growing child is in many respects encouraged to maintain a correspondence between what he says and what the world is like. He will learn to lie and to pretend, but hopefully he will distinguish between these and telling the truth and not pretending. Poetry may give more trouble. At primary school he may enjoy simple rhymes, especially those that he can say and sing, but is he then introduced to aspects of literary criticism before he can grasp the concepts involved – and then reproved for a lack of taste and sensitivity? Are standards of 'good' taste and refined sensibility presented with so little sensitivity to the present capacities of the listener that he can only become confused and humiliated? He can be confused because he fails to see the difference in the rules governing the referential and aesthetic uses of language. Questions about negative transfer across functions of language have not been examined. Certainly, in casual observations of some primary school children, we found scant evidence that children's reactions to poems went far beyond liking or disliking the story and sounds, although the instruction did go beyond this. If this is considered to be an exaggeration, empirical studies could quickly reveal the answers.

At some time it would be instructive to find out about the incidence of poetry and even prose reading in the adult population. Figures in the *Plowden Report* (Central Advisory Council for Education, 1967) suggest that, for large sections of the population, books do not have much significance: 18 per cent of families have no books in the home, 11 per cent between one and five – 56 per cent of the families of unskilled workers had fewer than six books (p. 116); in 32 per cent of families neither parent had belonged to a lending library within the previous ten years. Since children are avowedly educated to enjoy poetry and prose writing, some explanations of the relative unresponsiveness of the adult population to these pleasures should be sought.

Psychologists have not invested much effort in the study of what linguistic features of speech and writing are judged beautiful and pleasing rather than ugly and unpleasant. At least one symposium has brought together linguists, literary critics and psychologists (Sebeok, 1960), and while textbooks in general and experimental psychology omit entries under 'beauty' in the subject indexes, social psychologists are pleased to include the study of aesthetics within their current *magnum opus* (Child, 1969). In a society where increases in leisure purport to be imminent, the aesthetics of the language game, both everyday and professional, are obvious candidates for research work.

Encounter regulation

Goffman (1963) and Argyle (1969) in particular have recently opened up this problem lying at the heart of social psychology: how do two people initiate an interaction, maintain and close it. Several lines of research have been sparked off, including Schegloff's (1968) analysis of the sequence rules governing telephone conversations and Kendon's (1967) work on how people switch the conversational roles of speaker and listener. In many situations, non-verbal as well as verbal cues are relevant to these activities, and role relationships will be relevant to the choices of forms made.

Any language will probably have a finite number of items that can be used to attract attention, to greet, and to take leave, and there will be norms relating to the order in which events should occur, which items go together, and what choices of particular items mean. 'Hallo Jane' may occur in different situations from 'Jane Hallo!'. 'Watcha sir!' may be an uncommon compound greeting, while 'Watcha!', 'Hi!', 'Hallo!' and 'Good morning!' may convey different meanings. In the switching of conversational roles, direct questions, the use of intonation in unfinished sentences, and head and eye movements may serve to help switch roles smoothly. The use of these devices will be evaluated not only in terms of whether encounters occur and proceed smoothly, but also in terms of appropriateness to the role relationship of the participants.

In this case both selection of alternatives and sequence patterns have been studied to a minor degree, as discussed in chapter 7.

Performative utterances

Austin (1962) introduced a distinction between performative and constantive utterances, the latter often being used to assert propositions (called referential here) and about which one can pose questions of truth and falsity. Performative utterances do not report and are not true or false, but their very utterance is, or is a part of, the doing of an action – within a certain context: they enable a speaker to do rather than to say something. Austin's examples of ship-naming, betting, promising and marriage contracts are elaborated into a special theory of the ways in which these utterances can fail or succeed. The special theory grows into a more general framework of five general classes of performatives: verdictives, exercitives, commissives, behabitives (a shocker this!) and expositives.

It is easier to quote than to give a précis:

The first, verdictives, are typified by the giving of a verdict, as the name implies, by a jury, arbitrator, or umpire. But they need not be final; they may be, for example, an estimate, reckoning, or appraisal. It is essentially giving a finding as to something – fact, or value – which is for different reasons hard to be certain about.

The second, exercitives, are the exercising of powers, rights, or influence. Examples are appointing, voting, ordering, urging, advising, warning, etc.

The third, commissives, are typified by promising or otherwise undertaking; they commit you to doing something, but include also declarations or announcements of intention, which are not promises, and also rather vague things which we may call espousals, as for example, siding with. They have obvious connections with verdictives and exercitives.

The fourth, behabitives, are a very miscellaneous group, and have to do with attitudes and social behaviour. Examples are apologizing, congratulating, commending, condoling, cursing, and challenging.

The fifth, expositives, are difficult to define. They make plain how our utterances fit into the course of an argument or conversation, how we are using words, or, in general, are expository. Examples are 'I reply', 'I argue', 'I concede', 'I illustrate', 'I assume', 'I postulate'. We should be clear from the start that there are still wide possibilities of marginal or awkward cases, or of overlaps (Austin, 1962, pp. 150–51).

As one would expect from a philosopher of Austin's calibre, he proceeds to offer extensive examples of each and systematically follows Aristotelian tradition by attempting to specify the similarities and differences between each and every category. In several ways Austin's is a model of how a careful philosophical approach can set the conceptual framework within which a behavioural scientist might proceed to conduct his investigations. All that is surprising is that no behavioural scientist has taken advantage of Austin's pioneering.

In terms of linguistic features it is possible to be relatively specific about some of the characteristics that performative utterances must have to be in order. The major necessary condition is the use of one of the semantically appropriate verbs. Austin notes, however, that no case can be made out for the pre-eminence of any single simple obligatory grammatical structure of the general form 'I promise you I will come tomorrow!' To be successful, an utterance does not have to use the first person, the 'you' does not have to be explicit and can be realized as a third person pronoun or proper name, there is no necessity to use the active indicative present. However, as Austin adds, *all* performative utterances can be restructured to the above form without loss of meaning, if we append explicit reference to who the persons are. He notes parenthetically that the word 'hereby' can always be inserted into a performative utterance. He could have added that the relevant verb must always be used to link two persons or the actor and an object of whose identities there must be no doubt. As far as I can see the indicative verb must normally be in the present tense, and only in rare instances like 'It's dangerous. You have been warned', would we accept deviations from this.

In terms of Ervin-Tripp's criteria, the rules of substitution for performatives would need to specify the selection of semantically appropriate verbs and agents, possibly with a finite set of alternatives, much like that initiated by Austin himself. Co-occurrence rules will dictate that all of several units be present, referring to a performer, a receiver, a 'performative' verb and an instantiation of what is being done in this way. Sequence rules will include reference to a prior establishment of the necessary conditions for the performative act to occur, will demand of verdictive utterances, for example, that the utterance precede any outcome.

This sort of analysis neatly exemplifies the points made earlier, that an approach to the connections between social behaviour and language is unlikely to succeed if one tries to rely solely on a structural analysis. Promises, verdicts and ship-naming are to be evaluated as binding, effective or otherwise successful when values of contextual variables are set appropriately and one or more verbal events occur. We can specify some clear cases of grammatical structures obligatory in certain contexts, e.g. court verdicts and marriage services, but in others various structures may be used, provided that they employ a semantically appropriate verb uniting an unambiguous personal performer with an unambiguous person or object. That linguistic structure can be a basis for dispute as to whether a performative utterance had been successfully made indicates that it too can have a significant role to play.

Austin also observes that, although some utterances are clearly performative and others clearly not, there are others which are ambiguous. This is not surprising. His search for unequivocal criteria of demarcation probably rests on a mistaken view of how language works (see this book chapter 8).

Regulation of self
Behaviour and affect

Unlike speech regulating the behaviour of others, that which is used to control one's own behaviour has no unique label. 'Talking to oneself' is inadequate, both because it might be premature to eliminate from consideration covert as opposed to audible speech, and because simple talking may involve other functions such as encouraging oneself (affective instrumental) or giving a commentary of ongoing action (referential).

While there have been studies of this regulatory function in developing children (e.g. Luria, 1961), adults have been left alone. There are no reported studies of how housewives attempt to control their cake-baking or gardeners their rose-pruning. We cannot say with what frequency 'talking to oneself' has an apparent instructional component and, if it has, what its formal characteristics are. This is particularly unfortunate. It would be illuminating to know just what form the grammatical structure of the speech takes. Does it simply omit explicit references to features of the environment already understood, and therefore involve an extreme degree of contextual presupposition? Or is it 'telegraphic' in the ways in which the speech of very young children is, that is omitting as many function words as possible and relying on the order of selected lexical items to convey the essence of the message?

Without the necessary empirical evidence it would be hazardous to venture guesses about what differences found might mean. Could it be that the structures are commonly intermediate forms between the 'deep structures' (Chomsky, 1965) and their ultimate vocal realization? With so little knowledge of the facts of the matter we cannot readily offer answers to questions about any possible increases in efficiency a person might achieve through overt speaking to himself.

Studies with young children have led Luria to suggest a three-stage process in the development of the regulatory function: an initial one in which speech has no relevance, a second in which it accentuates the vigour of an ongoing activity, and a third in which the semantic value of the language units used becomes relevant. For example, a child at the intermediate stage with his hand poised to push a button will respond positively whether he says to himself 'Press!' or 'Don't press!', and while 'Press twice!' will yield one push, 'Press! Press!' will yield two. Claims to obtain such results (Luria, 1961; Lyublinskaya, 1957) date from a period when Russian psychologists were prone to present their supportive evidence in an illustrative and piecemeal fashion, so that other investigators could not critically examine the methodology or stages between premises and conclusions of arguments. Jarvis (1964), after most carefully piecing together fragments of information to recreate and elaborate one of Luria's most quoted investigations, found no evidence to support the results reported. Random results can be obtained by bad experimentation, but such a criticism would not appear to have substance in relation to Jarvis's work. The field itself is wide open. Klein (1964) has been able to show that speech to self declines with age, but that within that constraint, task-relevant mutterings increase and task-irrelevant speech decreases. There is variation among children, but high talkers do not appear to be either more or less successful at puzzles or button-pushing tasks than low talkers, although not all his results were random.

Both Jarvis and Klein suggest that certain parent–child variables may be relevant to how much children do talk to themselves, but they are not specific. Maybe highly dependent children being socialized out of close attachment to their mothers talk to themselves to reassure themselves: talking could substitute for whistling when you are afraid in the dark. Whether or not, and if so how much, speech-for-self is controlling affect rather than sensori-motor skills, and whether it works, we do not yet know.

We have already mentioned that we do not know what linguistic structures are used, whether or not there is a high incidence of imperatives and modal verbs, whether a large amount of presupposition and abbreviation is present or what.

As with behaviour, so it is with affect. We have no idea whether we can induce affective states merely by verbal auto-instruction.

Regulation of others
Behaviour

As with the regulation of encounters, our language does afford us lexical items like 'command' and 'request' which refer to activities involved in the regulation of the behaviour of others. Norms may require that among certain groups of people only a limited number of linguistic forms are likely to be efficient and polite, but the total range of possibilities for speakers of the language is likely to be greater. Soskin and John (see pp. 48–9) mention six verbally based ways of attempting to borrow a coat, but not all would convey the same meaning regardless of context or manner of delivery. People could evaluate these means not only in terms of politeness, but also in terms of probability of being understood. This is one reason for suggesting that it may be useful to distinguish between primitive and other linguistic forms. Imperative and interrogative forms used to give orders and ask questions and which include verbs of action as a focus are the immediately obvious candidates for primitive forms associated with controlling others. The modal verbs (must, need, ought, should) in combination with verbs of action would appear to be another set of primitives which enable a differentiation among reasons for the action being taken, although these enter a child's speech repertoire some time after requests and commands.

But in what sense are these forms more primitive? No doubt many a linguist would bring charges that this sort of view reveals a fundamental misunderstanding of the way language works. Utterances mean what people agree that they mean. It is true that a fine analysis of the constituents and their relationships in any proverb will not reveal the meaning of the idiom, any more than dictionary definitions will increase the chances of someone understanding 'Get up them apples!'. However we can trace the derivation of the use of 'apples', so that knowledge of the system of Cockney rhyming slang (stairs – pears – apples and pears – apples) reveals how a more primitive form is changed. The system could not work the other way round. The same style of argument can be brought forward for claiming that the use of 'Brrh!' or 'That coat looks warm' as indirect requests or commands – and we do call them 'indirect' – are derivatives. Their primitive functions are respectively to express your coldness or to make a statement about an attribute of a coat.

The issue of 'primitiveness' could probably be put to weak empirical tests if anyone wished to do so. One test would be to have a random sample of adult speakers judge what examples of each form meant. If a wide range of people judge the primitive form more unequivocally comprehensible, then its greater universality would suggest that particular sub-cultures have invented derived forms. Another test would involve comparisons of children at different stages of development. Provided that their utterances are based on the construction of sentences from their constituent elements rather than imitation of total utterances picked up from adults who use only the alleged derived forms, children should learn to use and understand primitive forms before they learn the derived ones.

Whether or not the verbal behaviour as a means of direct control is effective can be evaluated against the listener's comprehension, one strong test of which would be his obedience or disobedience. Reasons for not obeying could stem from a variety of sources other than a failure to understand, while failures to grasp the commanding force of some of the indirect forms mentioned by Soskin and John might indicate an ignorance of norms peculiar to a sub-culture. It would in fact be interesting to know whether or not some of the indirect requests can be readily discriminated from the forms having the more obvious function, e.g. does 'Brrh!' as a comment differ from 'Brrh!' as a request by virtue of non-verbal, para- or extralinguistic features?

Affective states

There is a range of activities which are intended to have effects upon the emotional states of others, variously labelled joking, jibing, warning, titillating. There are set forms for some of these activities, so that it would be possible to categorize jokes by their formal characteristics (riddles, shaggy dog stories) and semantic features (sick jokes, lavatory jokes). Psychologists have attempted to classify types of humour and link these to personality dispositions (see Flugel, 1954), but this work has not been pursued, and the social significance and linguistic features of jokes remain unexplored. Similar points may be made about other affective instrumental activities. A cursory consideration suggests that we would evaluate these activities in terms of their affective consequences. Do people recognize the intentions and are they amused, hurt, frightened and aroused? The almost total absence of any work in this area is an extraordinary omission. With a comedy conscious society devoting much of its time to watching and hearing the rampantly unfunny, at least the humour side of affective control might have appealed to some research student.

Expression of affect

One set of vocal features often ignored in teaching second languages are the indigenous forms of grunting, snorting, laughing, and enthusing. In so far as these expressive features are not unmodified innate responses to certain stimuli, then they are linked to or are part of verbal behaviour. The various expressive noises are perhaps minimal forms of utterances which can use words in exclamation or swearing, but their variety and efficacy remain unexamined.

Characteristics of emitter: marking of emotional states; personality and social identity

A person's speech may indicate how he is feeling, what sort of personality he has, who he is. Certain speech patterns are indicators of demographic characteristics such as age, sex, occupation, amount and type of education, nation or region of origin. There may also be links with personality, that is, relatively enduring characteristics referred to with words like intelligence, extraversion, neuroticism or psychotism. There are paralinguistic and linguistic features that signal ongoing emotional states. For social identity, although we cannot at present describe regional accents with great precision, a trained and well-informed phonetician can apparently emulate the example of Professor Higgins, at least to the level of county and town in England and can probably carry his detection more finely still, provided the necessary information is available. Grammatical and lexical choices, along with peculiar meanings for special structures and items may similarly contribute to identification, although precise details have not been tabulated. The casual observations of Nancy Mitford were expressed as distinctions between U and non-U English – the lexical choices of glass/mirror, pudding/sweet, lavatory/toilet, napkin/serviette and others marking off the lower middle class from those of a higher station. Unfortunately once the distinctive features are exposed, people aspiring to a certain identity may be able to incorporate them into their speech. Speech may reveal preferred identity as much as real identity, but here our concern is with noting relationships between the verbal and non-verbal rather than with deciding whether wolves are wearing their own clothes.

Speech is only one source of information for social identity. Static features such as physical characteristics, clothes and posture, dynamic features such as movements and gestures can also convey information. Speech as a marker of identity has been analysed so far only in terms of selections made, and not at all in terms of co-occurrence or sequence (see chapter 1). Similarly with personality and emotional states (see chapters 4 and 5).

Role relationships

Role definition is separated from marking of social identity. Identity marking in a two-person encounter may be relevant to the form of the role relationship which develops, but the relational markers themselves are likely to be quite different. As we shall see, particular relationships of kinship, familiarity and power are marked by the rights and obligations to use particular forms of address and reference. Rights to command and the form of command appropriate to given situations may be linked to certain role relationships.

As well as being marked by the use of specifiable linguistic forms, certain role relationships may also be associated with rights to prescribe what is and is not appropriate verbal (and non-verbal) behaviour utilized for other functions. For example, a question from a child intended to elicit information about a factual matter may be used by a parent or teacher as an opportunity to show authority. A classical instance is Petruchio's demonstration that he has tamed the shrew Kate by having her pronounce in quick succession that the moon is the sun and:

But sun it is not, when you say it is not;
And the moon changes even as your mind
When you will have it nam'd, even that it is.

The significance of such activities in the socialization of children is taken up again in chapter 9. As with addresser marking, studies have been concerned mainly with the selection of alternatives rather than co-occurrence or sequence. (See chapter 6.)

Reference – communication of propositional knowledge

Inevitably we arrive at the function most commonly offered at the head of the list, and the one that has probably been accorded most attention.

The primitive linguistic form is the declarative sentence used for making statements. We have no immediate need to worry about what truth or falsity might mean; nor is it necessary to go beyond an assertion that true statements are distinguished from false ones in that they correspond in some sense to features of the non-verbal world. It is perhaps worth noting, however, that the *tests* by which this correspondence is evaluated will differ from one sphere of knowledge to another and the work of philosophers has repeatedly pointed to this mistake, although not always deliberately.

In an early influential work Ayer argues:

If a sentence makes no statement at all, there is obviously no sense in asking whether what it says is true or false. And we have seen that sentences which simply express moral judgements do not say anything. . . . They are unverifiable for the same reason as a cry of pain or a word of command is unverifiable – because they do not express genuine propositions (1936, p. 108).

And:

The fact that people have religious experiences is interesting from the psychological point of view, but it does not in any way imply that there is such a thing as religious knowledge, any more than our having moral experiences implies that there is such a thing as moral knowledge. The theist, like the moralist, may believe that his experiences are cognitive experiences, but, unless he can formulate his 'knowledge' in propositions that are empirically verifiable, we may be sure that he is deceiving himself (1936, p. 120).

'Truths' of logics, 'truths' of science, 'truths' of morals, 'truths' of aesthetics and 'truths' of theology may not be verifiable through the same means. Not all knowledge is necessarily available for expression in verbal form at all, but where statements are made it is possible to inquire into their truth value. The means by which we come to decide whether or not to accept a statement as true or act as though it is true will differ with the types of knowledge.

In the realm of logics we inquire into the validity of arguments arising as deductions from certain invented postulates. Since the whole system is formal and symbolic there are no problems of checking correspondence with a non-verbal world. Morals and aesthetics represent universes of discourse where claims of an empirical nature might be made; theology certainly does. While we may demand that rules of logics apply to arguments within these realms and that their claims do not conflict with empirical knowledge, their basic postulates will rely upon tests other than those typically used by scientists.

Scientists have formulated rules by which we can at least establish whether propositions are appropriate claims about the nature of the non-verbal world, although in everyday discourse we very often have a sufficiency of shared experience and assumption not to have to question the veracity of statements made. Individual statements based on declarative forms can be strung into sequences to give arguments, into lists or hierarchies to yield classificatory systems. They can be used in problem-solving, in analysis, process and synthesis. We have many lexical items referring to activities based upon the organization of statements into systems. Much of our knowledge may well be *stored* in terms of the coding system afforded by language and can only be *transmitted* to others through the medium of language.

There is no chapter on this function *per se*, although in chapter 8 the issue is raised of the possibility of this use of language being accorded a low order of priority in some social groups, so that utterances intended to have some referential relevance may be decoded as attempts to control behaviour and affect or as conformity to norms.

Instruction

Language is used as a medium of instruction for both verbal and non-verbal skills. We may well find eventually that language used for instruction has distinguishing characteristics, but these are not immediately obvious and unique, and to discuss the basis of evaluation thoroughly would require an assessment of the total role of language in learning. More narrowly, knowledge transmitted will, if expressible in verbal form, be evaluated in terms of truth or falsity as with the referential function; but certain basic points can be made about more general evaluative problems because, although appearing to be platitudinous, they are sufficiently ignored in practice to merit assertion. The efficacy of verbal instruction in learning situations will vary with the character of what is being learned, who is learning, who is teaching and what other resources are available. We have already implied that in the teaching of English literature, children may often be expected to grasp principles and use them when these are beyond their current levels of comprehension. The Nuffield Science and Maths projects in schools are designed to ensure that empty verbalism should not extend too far ahead of experience necessary for understanding.

To simplify the issues, we may think of a hierarchy of tasks differing in the significance that verbal instruction might have for learning. At one extreme would be learning based on a classical conditioning paradigm. Here, where the problem is construed as one in which a conditioned stimulus (cs) comes to substitute for an unconditioned stimulus (ucs) for the evocation of a conditioned response (cr) very similar or identical to its unconditioned predecessor (ucr), the traditional procedure of repeated, appropriately spaced trials with optimal relations of contiguity in the presentation sequence cs/us appears to be a necessary condition of the learning taking place. The cs could be a verbal signal; verbal instruction might facilitate attention to relevant variables in the situation; but the trials cannot be avoided. It sounds obvious, but is not always treated so. Effort is still expended on talking a 'conscience' into delinquents, but if the operation of 'conscience' is essentially aversive conditioning with an affective basis involving the autonomic nervous system (Eysenck, 1964), chat is futile.

Similar considerations will apply for instrumental conditioning of responses and the building up of stimulus response chains, even when these are assembled into complex sensori-motor skills. Although complex skills may involve principles of organization and flexibility, the elemental constituents will have required practice.

Verbal instruction may assume greater significance in teaching complex skills to learners who have already established a degree of mastery over language and many of the constituent motor units. Not only can verbal instruction be used to draw attention to what is relevant, it can also be used to give knowledge of results, i.e. potentially corrective feedback. Additionally the regulatory function of language may be exploited. Verbal correlates may form the basis of the storage system for retaining some aspects of the knowledge; whereas repeated trials may be both sufficient and necessary conditions of learning simple skills, for complex skills they may be a necessary condition only. Verbal instruction may have a facilitatory role in simple learning, although be neither a sufficient nor a necessary condition, whereas it may be a necessary condition of learning complex skills. We may note, however, that all learning of non-human animals in their natural state is achieved without the use of language and hence we may well argue that in so far as animals achieve solutions of complex problems, the mastery of language as a coding system is not necessary. It will depend on how complexity is defined, and attempts at generalizations without specifications of details are likely to be uninformative.

For the mastery of the traditional subject topics in secondary schools or higher educational establishments, verbal instruction will be a necessary condition of a mastery of the concepts involved, their combination in principles (or laws) and their application in problem-solving. Appropriate non-verbal experience will also be a necessary condition of attaining the mastery. A specification of optimal arrangements of verbal and non-verbal experience will vary with what has to be learned, what the characteristics of the learner are and what resources can be deployed in the learning situation, but these problems constitute a major area of investigation in themselves (see de Cecco, 1968). A special sub-class of behaviours of immediate interest is instruction in the language skills themselves; the present focus of inquiry is upon grammar in young children – and this is a sufficient hot-bed of controversy for us to omit anything but a passing reference (Slobin, 1971).

Inquiry

Language is used for the transmission of meanings and, although in one sense all such communication is didactic, it is probably useful to distinguish between the explicit teaching or instruction function on the one hand and merely using language to communicate on the other. Likewise, just as these are overtly instructional uses, so there are overtly correlated inquiry ones. Questions can be expressed in several ways, the most obvious verbal forms utilizing inversion of the word order of a declarative form, with or without the introduction of a special initially positioned 'wh' interrogative marker or declarative form with a question intonation pattern (see Robinson and Rackstraw, 1972, for a fuller exposition).

As with instruction, the efficacy of verbal forms of questions will vary with the problem in hand and much else beside, and there will also be once more a special sub-class of questions relevant to all other functions of language. On a narrow basis questions can be evaluated in terms of their success at filling the gap in knowledge indicated; on a wider basis we would apply the referential criteria of truth and falsity to the possible answers that the question could acceptably evoke. If an answer could not be evaluated in such terms the question is improper.

Metalanguage functions

We have already noted that language can play a role in instruction and inquiry about itself in relation to various functions, but this refers only to the applied end of the discipline known as linguistics. No doubt a case can be argued for treating the function of a language to talk about language as differing in some important ways from the languages generated to talk about mathematical, sociological or biological problems. Whether or not there are problems peculiar to linguistic science we do not know – peculiar that is, in some sense other than those of material studied, perspective adopted or methodology and technology utilized.

But language is strange in a more general sense in that it has a capacity for growth. While knowledge in the physical sciences can grow, this itself being expressed in symbolic form, the raw data themselves do not change. Discoveries are made and concepts invented and related to describe and explain these constructions of experience. Such a constraint may not apply to much of behavioural science, including linguistics. New concepts and terms to refer to them can be invented, new rules of combination to express new meanings can be introduced, leading to changes in the raw data for linguists to handle.

What the consequences are of this feature of the system is difficult to conceive. Certainly one implication is that theoretical frameworks of description and explanation may have only temporary utility for reasons rather different from those that render comparable frameworks in the physical sciences temporary. And this arises because the very data themselves are under human control in the one case, but not the other.

4 Characteristics of Emitter:
Marking of Emotional States

Introduction

In our everyday encounters we make judgements about the states and conditions of other people and we make available information for others to make judgements about ourselves. We may announce these states with exclamations like 'Oh how great to be alive this fine spring morning!' as we leap out of bed radiating joy. We have a variety of grunts, murmurs and sighs whose meanings are as yet unexplored. We may offer direct reports: 'I am very happy'. Such utterances can, of course, be intended to achieve a state rather than express it, the value of acting to achieve such ends still being a matter of unknown power. They may also be self-deceptive or intended to deceive others.

At present the professionals know little more than the amateurs in this area. Grunts and sighs have not been classified nor have the occasions of their occurrence been described. We do not know what sort of people in what situations do or are prepared to announce what they are feeling. Nor do we know to what extent such reports and exclamations have been encouraged or discouraged by others. It may well be that in our particular society adults are discouraged from announcing some emotions in some situations and they are required to pass information about these non-verbally. Society clearly does not discourage comment on emotions to such a degree that our language lacks words to refer to such states.

Just as the announcements of states may be direct or allow a strong inference from a verbal utterance, so the lexical items that we can utilize may be usefully divided into those which focus attention on the state *per se*, but which have implications for behaviour (e.g. 'happy', 'angry'), and those which focus on behaviour and attitudes to others (e.g. 'friendly', 'hostile'), but imply the concomitance of emotional states. The vocabulary of the English language in this area is not very well organized, arising as it has without rigorous definition or validation. We are not even clear as to which of the words available refer to emotions as opposed to other categories of states or experience. There is no reference book which presents a diagram showing the relationships between words of emotion, their similarities and differences; neither is there much information as to whether the different words correspond to different states. Wherein lies the difference between contempt and disgust or joy and happiness? Are they associated with different physiological states or situational variables or a mixture of the two? Some unreplicated evidence points to associations between fear and the secretion of adrenalin, anger and the secretion of the hormone nor-adrenalin (Funkenstein, 1966), while other evidence (Schachter and Singer, 1962) shows that subjects misinformed about the effects of injections of a drug but put with a stooge who had supposedly had a similar injection tend to behave like the stooge and report moods similar to his. Experiments along these lines will help to lessen our ignorance, but in the meantime other types of study have begun to yield systems for classifying the use of emotional words.

Of several models extant, Osgood's (1966) megaphone shape probably offers the best fit to the data available (see figure 4). The data have been obtained mainly, it must be admitted, from judgements of subjects required to choose words appropriate to different facial expressions. Three dimensions are proposed: degree of activation, pleasantness, and degree of control over emotion, this last applying more to unpleasant than pleasant emotions. Particular words of emotion can then be located within this space in terms of the value ascribed to them on each of the dimensions. In so far as there is variation in usage across individuals, groups or subcultures, these could be described in terms of differences in values on the dimensions. It might be particularly instructive to play this game cross-culturally as Berlin and Kay (1969) have done with colour terms. They show

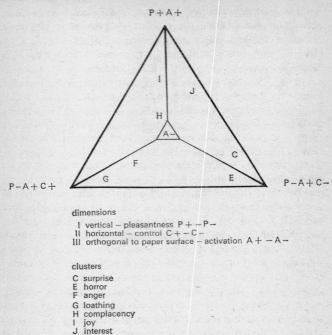

dimensions

I vertical – pleasantness P + – P –
II horizontal – control C + – C –
III orthogonal to paper surface – activation A + – A –

clusters

C surprise
E horror
F anger
G loathing
H complacency
I joy
J interest

Figure 4 Emotional expression solid (after Osgood, 1966, p. 23)

that, although languages differ in the number of colour contrasts distinguished by single words, there is a hierarchy of colours such that languages marking only a few mark those at the top. The study of the use of emotional words has been heavily confined to that of students in the United States. Osgood's model is also used to describe the developing differentiation of emotional words by children, his argument being that there may be a sequential order to development.

However, our immediate concern is not with the definition or classification of emotional states, although these issues require preliminary discussion. Presumably, increasing knowledge in such areas will eventually lead to changes in ordinary usage, so that our lexis of emotion increasingly comes to correspond to valid rather than imagined contrasts. In the meantime we know that people are able to agree sufficiently on the circumstances in which to use particular words to make it sensible to inquire into the rules they follow to achieve this degree of consensus. We also know that this consensus is not so universal, precise and accurate that there would be no more point in asking what rules they follow than there would be in asking how adults perceive that other people have two legs and two arms. Given such consensus as we have, how do language and its use function in the judgement of emotional states? In particular, what is the role of language as a source of information to others?

We often have more than one source of evidence. We may have information about the situational context; we may observe another's distance, posture, dress, gestures and face, as well as hear his voice and speech. In fact most of the early work was solely concerned with facial expression (see Osgood, 1966, for a summary) and only recently have the interactions of possible cues been examined (Mehrabian, 1968). On some occasions only voice and speech or written evidence is available. In telephone conversations, there may be informative background noises, while letters can offer cues from the orientation of the stamp on the envelope, the type of paper, the normality of the orthography and the old lover's dodge of a few discreetly sprinkled drops of tap water to show the tears of happiness or grief.

Here, however, we will content ourselves with voice characteristics and features of language use. Normally such voice characteristics as pitch, tone, volume and timbre, and their supra-segmental combinations in patterns of stress and intonation, are bundled together along with pauses, hesitations, false starts, repetitions and mazes into the categories of *paralinguistic* or *extralinguistic* variables – and then omitted from studies of language use. While this strategy might be justified, it is also true that all natural speech (and writing) will carry such features and hence they can only serve as cues for inference when speech is being emitted. If it is also true that speakers frequently avoid explicit linguistic reference to their states, the para- and extralinguistic features may be significant sources of information, especially if they are less amenable to voluntary control, as has been suggested.

We will first review work linking judgements of emotional states to voice characteristics in terms of whether or not such judgements can be made and if so how well. We will then examine what voice characteristics are associated with particular judgements. Finally, anxiety will be treated as a special case. Clinicians have particular interest in this state and signs of its presence.

Judgements of voice characteristics

The most systematic set of investigations into this area has been pursued by Davitz and his colleagues (1964), their interest arising from the practical needs of the clinical psychologist to diagnose and assess. If voice characteristics are differentially associated with emotional states, it should be possible to train clinicians to attend to and use such information.

The main strategy has been to ask subjects to make tape-recordings of semantically neutral messages like: 'I am going out now. I won't be back all afternoon. If anyone calls, tell them I'm not here.' Sometimes a prior text has been used to help the subject achieve an appropriate set, but generally the materials have relied on unaided simulation. Even with the weakness of design, for some thirty-seven messages involving ten different emotions, fifty-eight judges making independent assessments agreed with much better than chance expectation which emotion was being expressed, and their judgements coincided with the speaker's intention. The test–retest reliability of the judgement is reflected in a correlation of 0·74. The emotions simulated included affection, anger, disgust, fear and joy. The ease with which such a degree of independent consensus can be achieved clearly shows that at the least there are consistent beliefs about connections between emotional states and vocal characteristics.

Studies with such tape-recordings suggest that some emotions are more readily simulated and/or recognized than others. For example, Davitz (1964, chapter 8) found more successful identification of amusement, despair, fear and impatience than of admiration, cheerfulness, dislike or satisfaction. Likewise Levitt (Davitz, 1964, chapter 7) found fear more readily diagnosed than disgust or contempt. Levitt's investigation posed the further problem of the relationship between voice from recording as a source of information and face from motion film excerpts. Facial expressions gave 57 per cent correct identifications, voice gave 47 per cent and the two in combination 59 per cent. Levitt concluded that although voice is a significant source of information, it does not supplement facial expression significantly. However, his data imply that this is not the whole story, because for fear voice gave 74 per cent correct identifications, face 58 per cent, and voice plus face 73 per cent. This leaves us with too many unknowns to proffer solutions, but we can at least see the possibility arises that the vocal mode of expression may be associated more closely with some emotions than others. Its apparent *de facto* inferiority to facial expression may be also representative of a cultural bias towards the visual rather than the auditory channel. It could, for example, be true that the bases for inference from voice are more differentiated than those from facial expression, but that we are not aware of and hence do not normally use, such cues. Other studies by members of the Davitz group show that persons most effective in expression of emotions by voice are more efficient at recognition, and those who are most efficient at recognition using vocal characteristics are correspondingly better when relying on facial expressions, drawings, music, or metaphors (Davitz, 1964, chapters 3, 4, 7 and 12).

Davitz (1964, chapter 5) has also done some preliminary work which attempts to identify the characteristics of those most successful at these tasks. A wide range of scores on personality inventories, including measures of values, needs, traits and temperament, failed to yield significant associations. On the other hand a number of ability tests did. Verbal intelligence test scores, scores on Raven's Progressive Matrices (often viewed as a measure of non-verbal intelligence), and ability to isolate figures hidden in complex patterns of lines and colours all correlated positively with recognition of emotion scores.

Two other tests were also predictive. The somewhat inappropriately named Seashore Test of Musical Ability, which is intended to measure skills of discrimination in pitch, loudness, time (rhythm) and timbre, was associated with emotional sensitivity, as was the ability to express verbally what features characterize the expression of eight emotions (see Table 2).

These results are not interpreted as implying the greater the perceptual-cognitive skill, the greater the facility for the recognition of auditorially conveyed emotional expressions, but rather than certain levels of skill in such tasks are *necessary conditions* of being proficient. The tasks involve ability to attend to selected features, ability to discriminate values of relevant variables, ability to recognize patterns, and verbal ability. The list is hardly surprising, although it is interesting that an ability to express the relevant knowledge verbally is required; it might have been the case that the ability to represent the basis of the knowledge verbally would be unrelated to the skills of performance – that is that efficient performers could be unaware of how they succeed.

Cue characteristics in vocal expression

The data provided in Table 2 list some of the voice characteristics associated with inferred differences of emotional state. Loudness and pitch are generally correlated with the physical dimensions of amplitude and frequency of sound waves. Timbre is related to the shape of the cavities in the articulatory apparatus. Enunciation refers to the precision with which consonants are formed. Rate is self-explanatory. Inflection and rhythm both involve patterns rather than single dimensions or units and are reflected in relationships of pitch, loudness and rate.

Our present knowledge of the relationship between these characteristics and judgements of emotions is limited to say the least. The relevance of the patterns of inflection and rhythm was demonstrated by Knower (1941) who showed that emotions in speech played backwards were still recognized at better than chance levels, although with much less efficiency. Of course the patterning was still present but sequentially reversed and some

Table 2 Characteristics of vocal expressions contained in the test of emotional sensitivity (after Davitz, 1964)

Feeling	Loudness	Pitch	Timbre	Rate	Inflection	Rhythm	Enunciation
Affection	Soft	Low	Resonant	Slow	Steady and slight upward	Regular	Slurred
Anger	Loud	High	Blaring	Fast	Irregular up and down	Irregular	Clipped
Boredom	Moderate to low	Moderate to low	Moderately resonant	Moderately slow	Monotone or gradually falling	–	Somewhat slurred
Cheerfulness	Moderately high	Moderately high	Moderately blaring	Moderately fast	Up and down; overall upward	Regular	–
Impatience	Normal	Normal to moderately high	Moderately blaring	Moderately fast	Slight upward	–	Somewhat clipped
Joy	Loud	High	Moderately blaring	Fast	Upward	Regular	–
Sadness	Soft	Low	Resonant	Slow	Downward	Irregular pauses	Slurred
Satisfaction	Normal	Normal	Somewhat resonant	Normal	Slight upward	Regular	Somewhat slurred

more sophisticated manipulations are necessary to permit this conclusion. Knower also showed that when the fundamental frequencies (pitch) were highly attenuated in whispering, subjects could still do better than chance.

The possibilities of conducting systematic research in this field have been greatly enhanced by the technological advances in speech mutilating and synthesizing equipment. With the appropriate machinery to hand, changes in speech can be along defined dimensions. It is possible that skilled utilization of spectographic records will enable detection of emotions beyond the capacity of the ordinary listener as well as provide evidence as to relevant characteristics for him to attend to, but this does not reduce the desirability of seeing how the ordinary listener does make use of the underlying physical dimensions of vocal expression.

Davitz (1964, chapter 8) used selected tape-recordings of sentences uttered by subjects simulating different emotions and had judges rate each sentence on loudness, pitch, timbre, and speech rate in comparison with a sample of the speaker's ordinary neutral voice. The judges ratings were highly reliable in that they agreed very closely in their ratings on these aspects. They also rated the utterances on the basis of the three dimensions of 'meaning' defined by Osgood *et al.* (1957), namely, valence (good/bad), potency (strong/weak), activity (active/passive). Again judges agreed across these dimensions. While perceived activity was highly correlated with all four aspects of voice characteristics, valence and strength were not. A subsidiary investigation showing that erroneous judgements were more like intended emotions on activity than valence or strength, lends further significance to the dimension of activity as a major basis for judgement. It is regrettable that Davitz did not in fact check the associations suggested in Table 2 in the other study. It would have been more informative to know which vocalic features were associated with which emotion than how both related to Osgood's three dimensions.

Relationships between abnormal behaviour and language have been recently reviewed by Vetter (1969).

Anxiety as a special case

Anxiety may be treated as a special case for several reasons. The clinical world has a concern of sufficient strength about anxiety for there to be a relatively large number of investigations seeking to establish relationships between anxiety and both the linguistic and paralinguistic aspects of verbal behaviour. This work is seldom linked with the more general work on verbal behaviour and emotion, perhaps because there is some uncertainty as to whether to treat anxiety as an emotion. Sometimes it seems as though anxiety is unlabelled emotion – high on the activity dimension, perhaps being unpleasant because it has no clear directive component. It does not settle into anger and attack or fear and withdrawal; it leaves the organism in a state of conflict and tension. Certainly scores on self-report inventories of anxiety correlate very highly with scores on neuroticism scales (Edwards, 1957) and Eysenck views neuroticism as a state of high drive (1957). This is not inconsistent with those results which show that the highly anxious perform well-rehearsed overlearned behaviour with more vigour than the less anxious, but that irrelevant responses obtrude when learning is required or the responses are not overlearned. Clinical interest arises not only because anxiety is normally experienced as unpleasant but also because it is debilitating and at high enough levels renders a person's behaviour maladaptive.

Is this revealed in verbal behaviour? If so, is it found in both the paralinguistic and linguistic features? Oddly enough the vocal variables of volume, pitch, timbre and rate have not been studied, but interest has been focused on speech disturbances in the form of hesitations and various measures of influency.

Non-lexical speech disturbances

The clinical context has also stimulated investigations which have concentrated on signs of anxiety in speech. From his original observations Mahl distinguished eight categories of speech disturbance: 'ahs', sentence changes, repetitions, omissions, stutters, tongue slips, sentence incompletion and intruding incoherent sounds (Kasl and Mahl, 1965). It is maintained that these can be defined and observed with precision and

reliability (Mahl, 1956a) and with a reported frequency of occurrence of one disturbance for every sixteen 'words' spoken, equivalent to one for every 4·6 seconds of speech, sufficiently high for possible use as an indicator of changes in emotional states. Mahl's results show that 'ah' does not vary with various other possible measures of anxiety, but that a score of summed 'non-ah' items does. The incidence of 'non-ah' disturbances has been shown to vary with psychiatric ratings of changes in anxiety (Mahl, 1956b), palmar sweating and experimental inducement of anxiety (Kasl and Mahl, 1965). In a detailed analysis of a therapy session involving a single patient for nearly an hour (Mahl, 1963) argues a persuasive case for variations in the rate of emission of 'non-ah' disturbances being associated with anxiety provoking incidents. He also found a correlation of $+0·60$ ($p < 0·001$) between speech disturbance rate and statements of 'I can't . . .' and 'I don't know . . .', but not with negation in general. He notes 'although presumably very anxious, he [the patient] did not report this fact to Dr Deutsch; he did not say that he felt nervous, or upset' (1963, p. 99).

The situation is not this simple unfortunately. Various investigators report rather different results or no results. Alternative classificatory systems are available (Dibner, 1956). At the present time it looks as though there may be strong, but consistent, individual differences in the way in which speech disturbances and anxiety interact.

Mahl's finding that statements of 'I can't' and 'I don't know' correlate with 'non-ah' speech disturbances is supplemented in a pilot study of Rocksborough-Smith (1968), who counted a variety of 'filler' phrases in speech emitted under different conditions. Subjects spoke alone and with an interviewer, and in this second condition met with either agreement or disagreement on half of the topics discussed. Most filler phrases increased in incidence from the monologue to dialogue and there were significantly higher numbers of these when disagreement rather than agreement with opinions was operative.

Osgood and Walker (1959) assumed that suicide notes would be written under conditions of high drive and derived a number

of predictions from Hullian learning theory. They expected a high drive state to have generalized energizing effects as well as specific cue effects on habits of speech. The generalized energizing should lead to a simplification of speech, with more repetitions, a less diversified lexical content, fewer adjectival or adverbial modifiers and qualifiers and more 'familiar' words and phrases. Because habits have some effect on vigour, it is more likely that several habits may have identical strengths, the resultant interference and blocking leading to greater disorganization. The specific cue effects should be manifested in grammatical and lexical choices related to death, particularly in the form of self-destruction, and if there is more than one motive operating and they are in conflict there should be more evidence of this in suicide notes.

Two main comparative methods were used, one contrasting 100 suicide notes with ordinary letters and the other contrasting thirty-three genuine with forged suicide notes. For the tests of simplification six indices were used: the type/token ratio, the number of phrases and words repeated, the ratio of nouns and verbs to adjectives and adverbs, the incidence of adverbs of extremity (e.g. always, never), the ease with which words deleted from the text could be guessed correctly by further subjects, and the mean number of syllables per word. On all but the last measure the suicide notes differed significantly from ordinary letters, giving strong support to the original contention. However, neither index of disorganization gave significant differences.

For specific effects, suicide notes contained comparatively more references to distress than relief, more generally used evaluative terms, more positively evaluative assertions and more mands (statements demanding a response). There were no differences in time orientation, the suicide notes not showing an anticipated greater concern for the past. All three indices of motivational conflict showed up differences between suicide notes and ordinary letters. Verb phrases were more likely to be qualified by such additions as 'I tried to . . .' or 'I used to . . .'; there were more signs of ambivalence, e.g. 'but', 'if', 'should', 'because', etc., and more ambivalent evaluative assertions concerned with the self rather than with others. The 'forged' notes were written by students familiar with the results of the main analysis, and while graduate students did no better than chance in sorting the pairs into 'real' and 'forged', implying a successful simulation, the two authors could detect the differences (93·9 per cent and 78·8 per cent correct). Counting indices such as those above gave similar results to the main analysis.

It is unfortunate that this rewarding initial study has not been followed up.

5 Characteristics of Emitter:
Marking of Personality and Social Identity

Introduction

The borderlines between the marking of emotional states and personality on the one hand and personality and role relationship marking on the other are necessarily blurred. If anxiety states are chronic rather than acute, we may begin to refer to the sufferers as anxious people, thereby implying that anxiety can be a relatively stable personality trait. Similarly a sufficiently consistent predisposition to react with a similar set of emotional responses across a range of situations normally evoking a variety of reactions will shift peoples' judgements from state to person, from sin to sinner. There is nothing strange about this. They are problems posed from different perspectives, the first with an emphasis upon distinctions over time or conditions within a single individual, the second with a concern for generally found differences between individuals. We might naïvely expect to find that the relationships that exist between an individual's speech during unanxious and acute anxiety states are similar to those that are found between the speech of dispositionally unanxious and anxious people.

While some personality traits point inwards to emotional states, others appear to point outwards to role relationships. If we say someone is 'friendly' or 'aloof', we are providing information about their social behaviour with respect to other persons. Although relationships between judgements of 'friendliness' or 'superiority' and speech could be included in the next chapter, their incorporation here is justified mainly on the grounds that the investigators of such problems have set their studies in the context of person perception and inferences of traits from verbal and non-verbal cues, but no strong argument for this could be sustained. 'Interpersonal attitudes' seem to be an intermediate set.

However, there are other personality characteristics which traditionally at least have not been investigated within the context of changing states of an individual or in terms of role relationships. 'Intelligence' is one instance where the efforts have been directed towards individual differences. In this case too the language behaviour studies have been different for good practical if not scientific reasons. Whereas with emotional states it has been assumed that extra- and para-linguistic features of speech are the best starting point for study, with intelligence these have been ignored, and the main interest has been in the range and diversity of vocabulary items available (usually open form class) in relation to their semantic appropriateness and associates. For example, estimates of vocabulary size, tests of knowledge of synonyms and antonyms, and ability to spot similarities and differences figure strongly in intelligence tests. In recent years, tests have been devised which are less concerned to provide estimates of general verbal intelligence and more concerned to expose profiles of proficiency within language behaviours. The Illinois Test of Psycholinguistic Abilities (McCarthy and Kirk, 1961), based on Osgood's mediational analysis of language (Osgood, 1953), distinguishes between comprehension and production, utilizing both the oral and written forms of language. The linguistic unit of analysis remains the word rather than group, clause or sentence. How the bright and not so bright differ in their capacity to use these structures, or in phonological competence, voice characteristics, or in extra- and para-linguistic respects has not been examined.

It may seem unusual to mention 'intelligence' in this context of language characteristics and personality assessment, but this is only a paradoxical tribute to the pragmatic success of the test constructors and a criticism of their failure to retain the concept firmly under the aegis of personality theory. When aspects of intelligence need to be assessed, it is customary to select and give an already standardized test. The technology has advanced sufficiently for us to have access to procedures other than casual chats and weak inferences. And in everyday interactions should the need arise, alternative sources of evidence are available; we are probably more likely to make inferences about intelligence on the bases of people's ability to solve or discuss problems rather than rely on direct assessments of the speech they use. Whatever the reasons are, there has been little interest in the extent to which people could or do use speech characteristics for direct judgements. As we shall see, however, they are prepared to use speech characteristics indirectly; they are prepared to guess identity and make estimates of intelligence on this basis.

'Identity' figures in psychology in two ways, only one of which we are concerned with here. It is used in studies of the perception of the self, where in clinical settings we might talk about a person having a certain self image or losing his identity. Here, however, we focus on the related but different sense in which we, as observers of another, can ask questions about his social identity. It is far from obvious how this sense of the term identity should be defined in relation to personality, but it would seem to refer to what we treat as categorical rather than continuous variables. While a person may be more or less anxious or intelligent, he is either a man or a woman, an Englishman or a German. Identity appears to be used to refer to ascribed characteristics like ethnicity, nationality, region of birth and sex, and to achieved positions like doctor, Christian and Marxist. In this sense it presupposes the possibility of using a count noun (he is a . . .). Personality involves problems of describing and explaining attributes of individuals; terms used in personality have always an adjectival form that can be applied to individuals (he is . . .). Certain identities may be indicative of certain personalities. For example, the notion of a racial stereotype in its most extreme form allows its holder to draw inferences from racial identity to a whole range of personality traits – 'If he is an X, then he has attributes a, b, c, etc.' How this comes about is not of immediate interest; what is of interest, however, are the inferences from speech characteristics to personality traits, the inferences from speech to identity, and the inferences from speech via identity to personality traits. They are linked in this chapter because so many studies include both.

But to which identities and to which constructs in which personality theories are which language characteristics to be related? The task would be infinitely large if we were to relate systematically all inferences from all features of verbal behaviour to all those personality theories which have some measure of empirical validity – and we might reasonably ask what the point of setting out on such an enterprise would be. It would be blind empiricism and therefore not scientific. The same difficulties arise on the language side. *A priori* we might say that the whole range of extralinguistic, paralinguistic and linguistic features are potential carriers of information about identity and personality. The specification of which ones which people use with what degree of ecological validity again poses an absurd amount of data collection. It may be a fair guess that someone speaking Irish is Irish, that someone speaking English with an Irish accent is also Irish, that someone who speaks with utterances well above average in grammatical complexity is 'intelligent', that someone who says 'I am an anxious person!' is so, but we obviously cannot simply tabulate an infinite number of independent language and dependent identity and personality variables with a linking taxonomy, both as perceived and as true.

At the present time it is fair to say that we have no adequate theoretical framework or paradigm within which work is being carried on. Studies linking speech and personality have arisen out of applied settings, particularly clinical, educational and industrial, and they have arisen from casual or committed interests in how social class and racial status are signalled and interpreted. A number of investigations are almost certainly responses to an 'I wonder whether . . .' in the experimenter's mind – a faint echo of Bacon's original use of the word 'experiment'. As we might expect in the early phases of inquiry, investigators are still looking to see whether or not specific language variables are relevant to judgements of identity and personality, although there are signs of multivariate analyses appearing. In addition to this 'bits and pieces' approach within the field, the investigations themselves do not normally pursue their problems through. For example, we shall find that 'voice quality' affects personality ratings, but there is scant mention of just which features of voice quality are relevant and not very much concern with the reasons judges have for linking the two. If certain qualities of voice are thought to be indicative of low intelligence, do the judges make direct or mediated inferences? For example, do they operate with a rule which directly relates low intelligence to certain qualities of voice, or do they identify the voice as being of a lower working class speaker and derive the intelligence rating from their beliefs about members of the lower working class?

With certain reservations in mind we may proceed with a weakly representative review of work done. The first hazard is that there is no theoretical framework within which studies have been made, although there clearly are applied problems to which they are relevant. The second is that we are still at the stage of finding out what variables are relevant and are collecting this information in a relatively haphazard way.

This is regrettable, but also fairly inevitable. These probing pilot studies linking language and personality will eventually enable some person or persons to generate general laws referring to observed regularities which can then be further evaluated empirically. It is also likely that these descriptive laws will constitute a challenge that will eventually lead to explanations and theories.

Here we limit our coverage to examples of the role of speech as a source for judgements of personality. To set later investigations of 'accent' in the historical and methodological context out of which they arose, we first mention work in which the speaking of different languages was used as a basis for inferences about personality. There is some preliminary discussion of what accents are and how people react to them before we examine the inferences people make from particular ones. There are a small number of studies which look at other features of language behaviour as sources of information for direct judgements of personality traits, and in a final section we see the beginnings of investigations which ask how important speech is, compared with other variables in personality assessment.

Language and personality

Lambert and his colleagues at McGill University began the explorations of judgements of personality in the context of Canadian English and Canadian French speakers (Lambert, 1967). Groups of judges were required first to listen to recordings of read prose passages and then to make ratings of the speakers' personality. Lambert in fact used the same bilingual speakers across languages and accents in what he calls the 'matched-guise' technique. This is intended to act as a general control for error variance, and while it does not cover the eventuality that speakers may change relevant voice characteristics other than accent or language and may change their personality traits as well when they switch, it does eliminate some serious sources of differences that would be present if various speakers were used.

In an early study (Lambert, Hodgson, Gardner and Fillenbaum, 1960) it was found that English Canadian speakers (EC) made judgements evaluatively biased in favour of speakers in their EC guises. They rated speakers in their EC guises as better looking, taller, more intelligent, more dependable, kinder, more ambitious and as having more character, than in their FC (French Canadian) guises. A comparable group of FC speaking subjects made similar judgements, except for kindness whose distribution was reversed; additionally they viewed FC guises as more religious. These initial studies have been extended to cover sex differences, comparisons of evaluations of French Canadian and European French, EC and FC evaluations in relation to learning the French language, and the ontogenetic development of differential judgements. Outside Quebec, results have been found with switches from American English to Jewish-accented English; Sephardic to Ashkenazic style Hebrew with Israeli judges in Israel; Hebrew and Arabic for Israeli and Arabic judges; and American Negro speakers and listeners.

As Lambert argues at least two generalizations can be made: recorded voices

effectively call out the stereotyped impressions that members of one ethno-linguistic group hold of another contrasting group. The type and strength of impression depends on the characteristics of the speakers – their sex, age, the dialect they use, and, very likely, the social class background as this is revealed in their speech style. The impression also seems to depend on characteristics of the audiences of *judges* – their age, sex, socio-economic background, their bilinguality and their own speech style (Lambert, 1967, p. 100).

There are unmentioned complications in these studies which may be weaknesses. With the matched-guise technique itself it would be interesting to investigate how the non-verbal and verbal behaviour of bilingual speakers varies with the language being spoken. There is abundant evidence that contextual variables of register are related to the language chosen for speaking (e.g. Ferguson, 1959; Fishman, 1968; Blom and Gumperz, 1972; Gorman, 1971). When an Englishman switches to weak French and candlelight, his dining companion will be surprised if the behaviours manifested are identical to those he displays speaking English while drinking tea with the vicar's wife. Lambert is necessarily right (by definition) that personality *per se* cannot change with language switching, but the traits likely to be manifested do. Hence the judgements may have a greater measure of genuine validity than the proponents of the technique would wish – it is an empirical question.

However, judgements may reflect subjects' best first and tentative estimates in the absence of other information, a point enlarged upon later (see p. 106). Some workers in the field of 'stereotypes' have failed to see these responses from the subject's point of view. Often a person in authority, the experimenter, simply demands that the victim tick off adjectives typical of certain ethnic groups. The victim can protest that this is a nonsense. The experimenter may then insinuate a delicate trap by agreeing with the subject, but suggesting that he fill it in anyway as best as he can. If the victim then complies, he can draw on what he knows about the stereotypes floating around in the culture to complete the questionnaire. He can still refuse, in which case his questionnaire may not be included in the analysis. My personal prejudice is that some such sequence of events is all too common in this particular field of inquiry.

A third question has been recognized by Lambert in the passage quoted. The language heard enables the subject to identify the speaker and it is the 'stereotype' associated with this identification that is reflected in the personality traits ascribed – it is a two-stage process. In one sense the speech stimuli are irrelevant, the identificatory tag would suffice to generate the same results. Hence the verbalness of the verbal behaviour is, in one sense, irrelevant.

Reactions to accents

Accent appears to have been of little concern to linguists – in fact of such little concern that it is frequently omitted from consideration in textbooks of general linguistics. It is often thought of in terms of variations in pronunciation associated with geographical regions, although social factors are also accorded relevance. An oversimplification of reality might encourage us to define accents as constituting variants of a language in which only the particular realizations of a proportion of phonemes are different, grammatical, lexical and semantic rules remaining the same. While this notion of shifts in phonetic realizations of specific phonemes allows one to conjure up, for example, two lists of phonetic realizations of the forty-five English phonemes, one exemplifying typical Dorset and the other typical Durham, the issue is more complicated for several reasons.

Spencer (1958) has argued that rhythm, stress and intonation are relevant as well as vowel and consonant quality, implying greater complexity at the linguistic end of the problem. Such comments appear to be based upon a definition of accent which presupposes that the everyday usage of the word has a peculiar utility – accent here referring to all those phonetic and suprasegmental prosodic features that distinguish speakers from different areas. It might be more useful, however, to argue that differences between Dorset and Durham involve shifts in more than accent alone, confining the definition of accent to phonetic shifts of vowels and consonants, and hence restricting its use to features of speech alone.

If accents are eventually defined with heavy reliance on

notions of geographically defined boundaries, two further difficulties will arise. Firstly, phonetic shifts will probably be found not to be discontinuous and dramatic. Variations will occur from street to street, village to village, in much the same way as there is a gradual shift from French to Italian across south-eastern France into Italy, with mutual intelligibility between adjacent areas, but not over much greater distances.

Before resolving the problems of definition, we can do little more than review investigations which claim to use accent as an independent variable, but without an explicit mention of identity or personality as a possible mediating variable. Giles (1971a) has initiated inquiries into discriminations within rather than across accent, examining whether judgements about it varied with its 'broadness'. Although the answer was clearly affirmative, the way in which the judgements changed differed both across accents and across judges. There was some evidence of an increase in ability to discriminate with increasing age, but a concomitant decrease in willingness to discriminate evaluatively.

Giles (1970) has also opened up the question of what the perceived structure of accents is. Using the matched-guise technique with thirteen different accents, he asked a large number ($n=177$) of secondary school pupils differing in age, sex, social class and region of domicile about three aspects of accents which he labelled 'prestige status', 'aesthetic value' and 'communicative efficiency'. One of these labels gives grounds for concern. While 'aesthetic' was defined in terms of pleasant–unpleasant and 'prestige status' was described eponymously, 'communicative efficiency' was described in terms of how comfortable or uncomfortable subjects would feel if interacting with the accented speaker concerned. Comfort might be influenced by many factors, and if efficiency of communication was the focus of interest it is surprising that the variable was not described in terms of ease of hearing or understanding what was said. This could even be measured directly with tests of retention or shadowing. That the three aspects mentioned gave correlations of 0·67 with each other across the thirteen accents suggests either that the subjects could not discriminate between them or that the three happen to co-vary empirically – at least in this study. That the latter point of view has some validity is implied by the ratings for what was called 'affected received pronunciation' which occupied second rank for prestige status, but eleventh for the other two.

Wilkinson (1965) has suggested a three-tier hierarchy of status in England, with received pronunciation (RP) and some foreign accents at the top, accents of the Shires and Celtic fringe in the middle, and industrial urban accents at the bottom. Giles's data are fairly consistent with such a view: RP certainly achieved first rank on all aspects and Birmingham came in a very lowly position on all three. It is unlikely that the judgements were wholly independent of a prior recognition of the accent concerned, since substantially similar and highly correlated results were found when the children were simply given verbal labels rather than samples of read prose as a basis for rating.

Given appropriate, albeit expensive, machinery and time it should now be possible to extract the characteristic features of accents from both articulatory and acoustic perspectives. Such work could then form the basis of more detailed inquiries into the features of accents that are relevant to judgements of hearers. Are purely aesthetic considerations involved, or are these affected by social factors and if so what are they? Perhaps judgements are heavily affected by communicative efficiency defined in terms of ease of decoding messages? Is it the case, for example, that accents assigned to the lower ranks in Giles's study are those used by speakers who tend to fail to articulate consonants clearly, particularly final and medial consonants, a not uncommon comment about the speech of lower working class children, so that his data represent a compound of accent and inarticulateness? It may be that ease of discrimination is also a function of the accent variant of the speaker – or his familiarity with the problem of listening to particular accents. Suitable experiments could reveal whether or not this is so.

These issues are socially important as well as psychologically interesting. As Bernard Shaw illustrated and Giles has shown, one variety of accent has achieved especial status in England even if its actual title of 'received pronunciation' has itself little aesthetic appeal. This is the accent most widely encouraged as a way of speaking in schools; but if one talks with teachers about social class and pronunciation it is sometimes very difficult to highlight the distinction already made between clarity of phonemic distinctions and 'proper' pronunciation. When it is suggested that lower working class children have 'bad' speech because distinctions are omitted or blurred, it is not uncommon to obtain one of two reactions. The first is enthusiastic endorsement of the importance of R P. The second is indignation at this apparent threat to local culture and heterogeneity. Why people have difficulty in understanding the more significant distinction is itself of interest. It has already been suggested that the covariation of accented and unclear speech would repay study. It might also be worth exploring the relationship between phonemic sensitivity on both the auditory and motor side and relationships of these to difficulties with the visual-motor skills of reading and writing.

How the judgements of Giles' subjects came to be made is also of interest. Are the judgements of prestige, aesthetic value, and feelings of comfort mediated by some knowledge of who is likely to use such an accent and what his likely attributes are? Or are judgements of unpleasantness independent of such knowledge? If they are, are they culture bound or not? As we shall see in the next section we have yet to tease out how the judgements are arrived at. This present section has tried to focus on reactions to accent *per se*, but the work is obviously contaminated by an unknown amount of successful identification of the accents. In the next section this issue of identification as an intermediate stage looms larger.

Accent and identity

The extent to which the trained ear and informed head can locate voices in terms of nationality, region of origin, social class, type of education, or occupation has been assumed rather than investigated. Is Shaw's Professor Higgins a mythical beast, with his imputed facility for detection of identity from speech?

The most comprehensive studies in this area are those of Labov (1966, 1970). His analysis of phonological variation in

New York City speech by social class, context and other sources of variance was based primarily on his assumption that five speech variables would enable him to plot his charts. Without the aid of other items in the phonetic array, or of grammar, lexis, semantics or pragmatics, he was able to show how the proportions of realizations of these five – (r), (th), (eh), (dh), and (oh) – varied. From his results we may note that differentiation was a matter of proportions and not all or none. Further, using three to five variations in situation from casual to formal, he was able to reveal the interactions between social class and context. For example, social class differences in the pronunciation of (eh), (th) and (dh) were most pronounced when the style was casual, whereas the reverse was true for (r). With (oh), the lower working class (LWC) respondents over-corrected their pronunciation when the situation was formal, thereby outclassing the upper middle class (UMC) subjects. (Her English was too good, he said, which clearly shows that she is foreign.) (r) showed consistent but small differences by situation, (th) and (dh) large ones – with large class differences as well in these last two. In subsequent more detailed analyses Labov showed that whereas income as an index of social class had special relevance to (r), occupation was more closely associated with (th) and (dh). Sex and the ethnic group membership were shown to complicate the picture further. The richness of Labov's study can only be savoured by a detailed reading of it. The most sweeping generalization that may be drawn from it is that all relevant features of the social environment will be marked linguistically: a map of socially significant sources of variation can be matched by one of linguistically marked variation.

Accent, identity and personality

The sequence in this title is deliberate in so far as it reflects a succession of events which are unlikely to occur in certain other orders such as accent, personality, identity. We do not normally make inferences about personality from accent and then go on to guess identity. Whether people are prepared to make judgements on the basis of accents that they can in no way identify has not really been considered. In general the studies investigating these problems have appeared to assume successful identification.

Strongman and Woozley (1967) used a matched-guise procedure with Yorkshire and London (RP?) accents and required their student judges to assess the speakers on eighteen personality traits. It is reasonable to assume that subjects were able to identify these accents. The judges were divided into two groups – northerners and southerners. Northern subjects rated the Yorkshire speakers as being more good-natured, generous, kind-hearted, reliable, honest and industrious; southerners rated them as more serious, honest, reliable and less self-confident. This is very much a pilot study: 'north of Staffordshire' is a rather weak grouping of region of origin, while all the students were in fact attending a southern university. Cheyne (1970) compared similar judgements of Scottish and English speakers. The English rated the male English speaker guises as being more intelligent, ambitious, self-confident and more likely to be leaders. The Scots judged the Scottish voices as indicative of greater generosity, goodheartedness, friendliness and likeability. Giles (1971b) has suggested that this type of trait separation is compatible with Lambert's (1967) view that three broad groupings of traits are involved, epitomized by competence, integrity and attractiveness. Cheyne's subjects accorded the RP English speakers competence, while his Scottish judges assigned greater integrity and attractiveness to their own group. Giles included three accents, RP, South Welsh and Somerset, for ninety-six subjects to make inferences about eighteen bipolar traits. While he found that the RP voice was rated higher on five competence traits, this was not so for personal integrity and social attractiveness. South Welsh and Somerset were differently evaluated on these last two characteristics and the particular analysis used obscured possible differences between these and RP. These might have been extracted with an analysis of variance and it might have been preferable to have avoided the confounding independent variable of half the subjects coming from Somerset and half from South Wales. In another investigation, Giles (1971a) selected extreme groups in terms of answers to the British ethnocentrism scale (Warr *et al.*, 1967) and had them judge six accents. Highly ethnocentric subjects fairly consistently rejected the five regional accents more than the low ethnocentric subjects, but judged R P as more aesthetically pleasing than the low scorers.

In these studies and in Lambert's, the relevant speech characteristics used as a basis of discrimination appear to involve a two-stage process of inference, as Lambert himself has suggested. The speech characteristics enable the judge to apply an identifying label, which in turn has certain traits associated with it. If the mechanism of inference is of this kind, then presumably characteristics other than identifying accent could be substituted with no change in results, or even the direct label French Canadian, Scot, or Yorkshireman could be used instead. If this is so, then are we learning anything more than that judges have stereotypes of particular groups of people of which one feature is the language they speak or the accent they use when they speak? We learn that language or accent can be a sufficient cue for successful assignment of a speaker to a particular category, but we do not learn anything about direct links between speech characteristics and traits.

We might also have doubts about the stereotype. In these studies the judges are required to make ratings. They can refuse to do the task on the grounds that it is impossible without further information; they can call upon what they know about stereotypes of the character of particular groups; or they may actually hold the stereotypes views. As Argyle and McHenry (1971) have recently demonstrated, the so-called stereotype of bespectacled people being more intelligent is readily susceptible to elimination if further information is provided. A judged twelve-point difference in intelligence test scores attributable to spectacles from a 15 second video-recording was reduced to a negligible difference after exposure to a 5 minute video-recording. The original idea of a stereotype involved notions of inflexibility in the face of discrepant information. Argyle and McHenry gave very little more information, but it was sufficient to change the judgements. It is therefore questionable just what measure of predictive validity accents would have to trait judgements if supplemented by further information about the speakers. That people are prepared to make judgements about traits on the strength of hearing accents may be an artefact of the experimenter's design rather than an index of the subject's naïvety, or prejudice, or willingness to pass judgement on possibly irrelevant information.

This is obviously not the whole story however. Initial categorization of people on the basis of accent may lead to quick judgements about other people and may effectively preclude further interaction, and judgements can be less ephemeral than those found with Argyle and McHenry's sample. Gardner and Taylor (1968) had Canadian subjects listen to three versions of speeches on the topic 'What Canada means to you', all delivered in English, but with a French Canadian accent. In one version the interviewee made remarks that suggested he conformed to the French Canadian stereotype on six traits, in the second he gave evidence of having the opposite characteristics, in the third he avoided any reference to the traits. Subjects were also exposed to pooled judgements of four other subjects prior to making their own ratings, the pressures being directed towards the traits opposite to those presented by the character. The ratings tended to be polarized towards the stereotype end of the dimensions, except in the three conditions where all the available information contradicted the stereotype. Both message content and social pressure affected judgements significantly. Gardner and Taylor suggest that group identification does call up the stereotype and for judgements to be moved away from this, information must be inconsistent with the stereotype, i.e. the onus of proof is on the speaker to show that he does not conform to the stereotype. At least he can succeed in some circumstances. Studies of racial hostilities, however, show that he cannot succeed with all of the people all of the time.

Summary of inference problems

Figure 5 sets out the inference problems in diagrammatic form. Complete arrows indicate studies have been done on this sector of the inference process. Hatched arrows indicate studies have

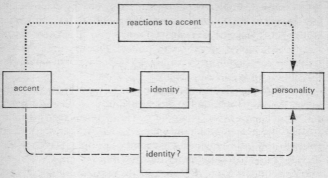

Figure 5 Inferences from accent

been done, but have not teased out the relevance of the possible mediating role of identity. Dotted arrows mark as yet unborn studies.

Prosody and personality

In one avenue of research Lambert and his colleagues have moved away from contrasts of ethnicity to studies of teachers' judgements of children. Brown (1969) has contrasted the speech characteristics of upper and lower social class French Canadian speakers and found among other things that, relative to the lower class, the upper class speakers articulate more clearly, use more intonation and stumble less over words. Frender, Brown and Lambert (1970) have subsequently studied these and other speech characteristics among lower class eight-year-old boys. Selecting only boys scoring above ninety on a non-verbal intelligence test, the investigators had the boys read a short simple passage which was recorded. A trained linguist, who was unaware of the nature of the study, rated these speech samples on pronunciation (both articulation and accuracy), speed, intonation (both amount and appropriateness), accentedness, voice characteristics (pitch and quality) and individual characteristics (nervous–confident; stumbling–fluent). Measures of scholastic achievement overall and verbal intelligence test scores were also available.

For the main analysis boys were divided into the two groups of high and low achievers. These groups did not differ in non-verbal intelligence test scores, but the high achievers were significantly higher on the verbal scores. They also differed in their speech characteristics: high achievers spoke more quickly, used more intonation and used it more appropriately, used a higher pitch and sounded more confident and self-assured than low achievers. With the possibility of explanation that the verbal intelligence test scores were directly associated with the speech characteristics, Frender *et al.* used a covariance par-tialling technique, but found intonation, pitch and softness of voice still associated with high achievement.

It is a little difficult to know how to interpret these results. One line of argument might focus upon the fact that the children were reading rather than speaking. While it is not made explicit that reading skills were part of the measure of scholastic achievement, there is a high probability that this is so. What does the poor reader of eight do in the reading situation? One guess would be that, faced by a task that is too difficult for him to accomplish overall, he will concentrate on specific features at a low level of linguistic organization, probably pronunciation. He might well decrease his cognitive load by speaking more slowly, a result significant in the first analysis and nearly so with verbal scores partialled out. Supra-segmental features of intonation would be sacrificed. He is not likely to sound confident, simply because he is not; again the attenuation of the effect in the covariance analysis gives some support to this line of argument.

The inferences to be drawn from this study are not clear cut. It may be that certain inadequacies in grammatical, lexical and semantic skill covary with inadequacies in speech characteris-tics, often as a result of general cognitive deficiency, and that therefore judgements based on the relevant speech characteris-tics have an initial plausibility in the absence of further incon-sistent information about the speaker. On the other hand, the speech differences found may be mainly a function of a response to the particular problem of reading when this skill has still not been fully developed. Just as Labov's (1966) studies show variations in the pronunciation of certain consonants with the casualness of the speaking context, so here pronunciation may receive attention to the neglect of other features.

That the speech characteristics found to differentiate between high and low achievers are used by teachers as a basis of judgement is suggested by a subsequent study. Seligman, Tucker and Lambert (1970) contrasted the relevance of examples of work, speech and face to teachers' judgements. Drawings and compositions rated as excellent or poor, photographs of faces rated intelligent or unintelligent, and reading voices rated as intelligent or unintelligent were presented in eight combinations for student teachers in their final terms to judge in terms of 'good student', privilege, intelligence, enthusiasm, self-confidence and gentleness. In a three-way analysis of variance, speech characteristics differentiated on all six judged attributes, while photos and compositions and drawings differentiated on three each. The interaction of voice and photograph was significant for the socially relevant traits of self-confidence and gentleness, but not on the competence attributes. The results did reveal interesting simple effects with, for example, photos being irrelevant to judgements if the voice is 'good', but affecting judgements of self-confidence if the voice is poor.

In the discussion the authors conclude:

One would have hoped that teachers, when evaluating a child's intelligence or academic potential, would have relied only on relevant information. Surely, drawings and compositions reveal more about a student's creativity and capacity for self-expression than a photograph or speech sample. Yet, the results showed that subjects considered voice when judging intelligence, and both voice and physical appearance when rating student capability.

The fact that subjects made serious and systematic judgements about students' abilities based on possibly irrelevant information, such as voice and physical appearance, is of great social importance (Seligman, Tucker and Lambert, 1970, p. 12).

Unfortunately, there are a number of assumptions here about what is and is not relevant, and how fixed such initial judgements are, as we have already seen.

Voice quality and traits

While we have seen that voice characteristics can be effectively utilized for judgements of emotional states, can they also be used directly for judgement of traits?

Hunt and Lin (1967) chose two passages from the materials of Markel and Robin (1965), one labelled 'death–hostility' and the other 'vocational–neutral'. Two speakers had agreed that one of these passages was 'like me' and the other not. They tape-recorded both the in-character and out-of-character passages. These speakers had also differed in their responses on twelve out of eighteen bipolar adjective pairs on a self-rating scale. Seventy-eight subjects heard the speakers' recordings and completed the same check list as the speakers. The first note-worthy feature in the results is that in-character and out-of-character passages had no relevance to the judgements; neither had the passages themselves. However, subjects did achieve considerably more than chance accuracy with both speakers. There was evidence that those judges who were accurate with one speaker were also accurate with the other, while sim-ilarity between self and speaker was irrelevant. The traits themselves differed in accuracy of perception: forceful–gentle, assertive–reserved, realistic–idealistic and bold–cautious were all identified accurately by over 80 per cent of the judges; only orderly–casual and agile–slow were perceived with less than 50 per cent accuracy. What is common to those traits judged ac-curately and how they differ from those not judged accurately is of obvious interest. It is suggested that affective conative traits are more easily judged than behavioural physical ones. It is also guessed that timbre, inflection and stress are likely to be qualities of voice significant for the judgements, but no supportive results have yet been obtained.

Another extralinguistic feature, hesitation, has also received some investigation. Lay and Burron (1968) selected the tape of a speaker who had shown a high rate of filled pauses, unfilled pauses and repetitions. These features were edited out from one copy of the tape. Separate groups of subjects rated the speaker on one tape only across forty-four trait adjectives, fifteen highly desirable, fourteen neutral, and fifteen of low desirability. They also made ratings on hesitancy and fluency, and anxiety, tension and nervousness. The judges discriminated between the tapes on fluency (but very weakly) and hesitancy, and the female judges did ascribe desirable traits to the non-hesitant and undesirable ones to the hesitant speaker. However, neither female nor male judges rated one speaker as more anxious, tense or nervous than the other.

Speech in interaction with other independent variables

Not only have the studies so far mentioned confined themselves to single aspects of language variables, they have also not included variables other than aspects of language as determinants of judgements. These restrictions are necessary in so far as investigators have limited objectives and resources. As Brunswik (1956) argued however, there are advantages in multivariate designs that allow all relevant variables to vary, but under experimental or statistical control. Only in this way can we eventually examine interactions of variables and build up a total picture of the content and processes of judgemental activities involved.

Two sets of investigations rather different in objectives and technology will be given, both concerned with attributes of personality directly related to interaction with other people, that is role relationships.

Argyle, Salter, Nicholson, Williams and Burgess (1970) used two independent variables intended to convey attitudes of superiority, equality and integrity: the content of oral messages and the manner of delivery, including voice, facial expression and physical posture. A superior attitude, for example, was signalled non-verbally by an unsmiling face with the head raised and a loud dominating voice, and verbally by telling the subject that there was no point in telling him about an experiment since it would be difficult for him to understand. Using videotaped recordings the experimenters presented subjects with all combinations of verbal and non-verbal cues and asked them to indicate the impression that the speaker made on them by checking off ten bipolar items on a seven-point semantic differential. With an ingenious if questionable statistical control, Argyle *et al.* calculated that subjects accorded over four times as much weight to non-verbal as they did to verbal cues as they shifted their judgements across conditions, this being particularly pronounced for the item inferior–superior, where the ratio of the variances overall was 21·7 to 1. The content of the messages had a significant effect on its own for six of the ten scales used, the non-verbal cues on all ten. If one asks how the two types of cue operate independently and in combination, then verbal content had a significant effect on the scale inferior–superior, but in combination with non-verbal cues this effect was eliminated. The authors claim 'that verbal cues only operate as multipliers – they can make an inferior non-verbal signal more inferior or a superior one more superior, but have no effect on a neutral signal and are ineffective when in conflict' (p. 230).

While Argyle *et al.* offer possible interpretations of their data in terms of innate patterns of communication, claiming that verbal content is not characteristically used for relaying interpersonal information (perhaps they are fortunate enough never to have been told 'I hate you!'), they omit one likely candidate. As they point out, face-to-face communications are multivariate, and when we are being sincere, proxemic (spatial), postural, gestural, extralinguistic, paralinguistic and linguistic cues will be in harmony, each having values that indicate the nature and state of role-relationships. When we have difficulty in defining the role relationship *vis-à-vis* another person or are trying to deceive him, that is, when we are putting on a performance, we have to control and monitor all cues presented. If we are well-versed con-men it may be possible to achieve total control. When we lose control which cues are least amenable to voluntary control? One hypothesis would be that the para- and extralinguistic features of speech are. That this might be the case is better illustrated in a second experiment from the same research group.

The first study was repeated (Argyle, Alkema and Gilmour, 1971) substituting a friendly–hostile dimension for superiority–inferiority. The results were very similar. Using the same matching procedures as before, the non-verbal cues (including voice) were calculated to be six times as influential as verbal cues. Two different patterns appeared when the values of the verbal and non-verbal cues were in conflict. When the verbal were friendly but the non-verbal hostile, the speaker was judged 'insincere'; when the verbal were hostile, but the non-verbal friendly, he was seen as 'confused'. That these judgements were not the other way round is relevant to the interpretation offered above that one set of cues is under a greater degree of voluntary control than the other. If we assume that a person is trying to give an impression of friendliness, failure on the non-verbal cues is judged insincere, whereas failure on the verbal content is judged confused. It is as though the subjects cannot explain why someone should make unfriendly remarks when the other cues imply a different attitude, so that they can assume only that he is confused. Subjectively too we may agree that the control of tone of voice and face is harder to achieve than control of verbal content.

From the point of view of a social psychologist of language behaviour, it is a pity that the experimenters did not divide their non-verbal independent variable in two, with variations of voice quality being manipulated separately from face and posture. The work of Davitz (1964) referred to in chapter 3 suggests that face alone is generally more powerful (within the confines of the values of variables used) than voice as a determinant of judged emotional state, but is this the same for traits relevant to role relationship?

It is noteworthy that Argyle *et al.* have chosen for their investigations indices of two dimensions closely related to those used by Brown (1965) to account for variation in the usage of forms of address and pronouns. The authors themselves do not explicitly draw attention to this, perhaps because these dimensions have become part of the woof and warp of social psychology.

Quality of speech has also entered into the accumulative series of investigations into determinants of social distance, friendship, admiration and evaluation conducted by Triandis and his colleagues (Triandis, Loh and Levin, 1966). (The notion of 'social distance' was introduced by Bogardus (1933) to refer to how close to themselves people like others to come. 'Closeness' was conceived as a psychological rather than a physical dimension, although there may be some kind of relationship between the two.) Triandis *et al.* employed two values each of four variables: race (negro *vs* white), belief (Civil Rights Bill: pro *vs* anti), dress (suit *vs* overalls), spoken English (grammar: good *vs* poor). Subjects were shown photos and played tape recordings of target people's comments about civil rights, and with this manner of presentation, it was thought necessary to vary voice quality for race and dress.

The pattern of results showed that while race was a determinant of social distance and friendship, belief related to both evaluation and admiration, dress related to friendship. Grammar of spoken English related strongly to all four dependent variables, accounting for over 70 per cent of the total variance; its effects were most prominent *vis-à-vis* social distance among those subjects who were liberal moderates, race being more important in extreme groups.

Just as Argyle *et al.* confounded voice quality with face and posture, Triandis *et al.* confounded voice with dress and race, so we are not that much wiser about the relevance of voice or language behaviour *per se* to judgements of other people. The grammatical variation introduced by Triandis clearly had a powerful effect. How this was mediated, however, remains available for further investigation.

Whither now?

The studies in this area could be grouped according to different principles, but one possible separation would be into three sections. How are speech characteristics reacted to in their own right? What language behaviour characteristics are empirically associated with aspects of personality and identity? How do people use language behaviour characteristics in forming their assessments of other people – and why, if the inferences are invalid?

Strictly speaking, the reactions of people to samples of language are not directly relevant to the heading of the chapter, but since these may well affect subsequent judgements, they may be included. What aspects of language are relevant to responses? Do human beings find a Birmingham accent aesthetically unpleasing if they are unaware of who it is that normally uses the accent (e.g. what do members of the Commonwealth feel about unidentified accents)? Are some accents spoken with a lack of phonetic clarity so that this makes them more difficult to decode which in turn decreases a listener's willingness to listen? These specific questions are but instances of the more general problems about the behaviourally significant aspects of speech from the listener's point of view. If these could be teased out, some of the issues about assignment of traits might be rendered more amenable to interpretation.

The Frender *et al.* and Seligman *et al.* studies both mention an educational concern that certain characteristics of speech may serve as an *irrelevant* source of information which teachers may use to differentiate between children in classrooms. It is a moral as well as a social psychological problem, but if we concentrate attention on the latter, we have to answer empirical questions about actual covariance of language and other behaviours. Lambert and his colleagues may well be correct in their interpretation that aspects of behaviour irrelevant to potential for intellectual and other development are employed by educators, but if the self-fulfilling prophecy is fulfilled, then paradoxically the argument that certain language behaviours are associated with educational attainments has a reasonable (even if unnecessary) foundation. *As a matter of fact* certain language behaviours may covary with other attributes in the adult population. The separation of those which are accidental (psychologically if not sociologically) from those which are linked in some other way would open up the notion of some speech attributes having high ecological validity.

Investigation as to how the current systems of inference operate (especially the invalid ones) has begun, albeit in bits and pieces. Some language variables have been used as independent variables both alone and in combination with other cues. These latter studies are perhaps particularly interesting in that they begin to move the stimulus characteristics back into the 'real world'. While human beings may occasionally have to make snap judgements about others on the basis of a brief telephone conversation or photograph, we can normally arrange for our inferences about others to be based on more intensive and extensive information. Psychophysical studies of the discriminations which can be made may inform us as to which physical dimensions of speech features can be used as a basis for inference about other characteristics of a speaker, but they may not tell us how the inferential processes work in everyday situations.

One line of approach would argue for the fruitfulness of the approach of the study of social behaviour adopted by Goffman (1963). Participant observation of the ways in which people do use speech variables as a basis for judgements is a neglected line of inquiry. The complaint against laboratory studies would not be that they should not be done, but that they run the risk of being premature. With a background experience of detailed observation of how speech is exploited in natural settings, investigators might also be less prone to constrain the behaviour of judges in such ways that artefactual results, in the sense they are misinterpreted, are generated.

6 Marking of Role Relationships

Introduction

We have mentioned that one function of language is to define role relationships. 'Role' is a commonly used term of varied definition, but often refers to the set of behaviours prescribed for or expected of a person occupying a certain position in the social structure. If we were to list terms like 'coal miner', 'priest', 'neighbour', 'friend', or 'father', we could quickly write down both general and specific behaviours we would expect occupiers of these positions to manifest. Different sub-cultural groups may have different definitions of what is appropriate behaviour for particular roles, and roles allow different degrees of individual discretion as to how they may be played; but always there are rules, written or unwritten, spoken or unspoken, general or specific, pervasive or peripheral, that govern the behaviour of a person as a member of a socially significant category.

Many activities are essentially non-social and how we perform these is up to us. If I wish to dig my garden with an eating fork I may. If I wish to paint my car with purple and yellow stripes I may. But there are other activities which require a second person to play the game as well. If I am playing tennis and my opponent golf, the game being played not only defies description, it ceases to exist. Similarly, if I march on to a parade ground and start giving orders that the troops do not obey, I am prevented from playing sergeant major. If I travel first-class in a railway carriage there may be certain behaviours necessary for inclusion in any group activities that may develop. I can easily become a first-class passenger by paying the fare, but I can only become a first-class passenger acceptable to other such people if they allow me to do so. A wise young mother on a long journey with a young child may elect to go first-class, but when the only other occupant looks round the compartment covered in signs saying 'First class', turns to her and asks, 'Is this a first class compartment?' the question is not a request for information. In such cases, acceptability may depend upon static features such as posture, clothes, hands and face, or dynamic features such as gestures and facial movements. And there is speech. As suggested in the previous chapter, the trained ear and the well-informed brain may be able to identify another person sufficiently quickly to take a decision as to whether to encourage or discourage further interaction. In the jargon – in any encounter between participants the language features used can define the nature and state of their role relationship. This is neither new nor profound. Everyday communication abounds in particular language forms associated with particular role relationships, and we both use these effectively and are aware of many. But oddly enough, if we watch ourselves and others more closely we can find relationships in which we experience difficulties because of a mismatch in the verbal and non-verbal aspects.

However, what is known at the level of anecdote does not constitute science. A list of incidents as examples will not by itself make up a system. We will need to organize the anecdotes. We will need to group them and offer interpretations in terms of general principles – and then test the validity of these interpretations in new instances, perhaps by simple observation, perhaps by the controlled observations called experiments.

Since the study of role relationships and the speech used to mark them has exemplified one common strategy of conducting research in a new area, this topic is treated in greater detail than some others in order to illustrate the methodology. This strategy is to delimit a very circumscribed problem and study it intensively in the hope that the principles which can be discovered there may have application in other areas.

In the study of role relationships and their verbal associates special attention has been paid to *forms of address* – what one person calls another and what this signifies. Given that the cultural possibilities allow an encounter to take place, what is conveyed by the acceptable use of one form of address rather than another? What are the rules governing the selection from among the available array? In our society the use of the title 'Sir' may convey a different meaning from 'Jones' or 'Mr Jones' which in turn may not be equivalent to 'Honey bun'. But what are the facts of the whole story? This particular problem has an advantage over some others in that what appear to be reliable and valid data can be collected fairly easily. We can examine our own usage and that of other people without much difficulty and the general principles exemplified should also emerge fairly readily. This is not over surprising since, if forms of address are one feature of a communication system whose efficiency depends upon convention, it is necessary that these conventions be generally known in the culture.

Forms of address

Two aspects of forms of address have been studied in some detail across several cultures using several different sources of material. Brown and Gilman (1960) concentrated on the pronoun system in those Indo-European languages which have two forms of 'you', summarily referred to as T (*tu, du, ty, tu, tu*) and V (*vous, Sie, uy, usted, vois*), while Brown and Ford (1961) have examined the usage of proper names. This work has been integrated within a social psychological framework by Brown (1965) and a sociolinguistic one by Ervin-Tripp (1969).

Somewhat exceptionally in the study of social behaviour the emergent story is clear, coherent, plausible and remarkably universal in its application through time and across cultures and languages. In part this consistency may be attributed to the reliability and validity of the data. It has already been suggested that people may be able to give accurate reports of forms of address used; indeed they must be able to do so if the conventions of this communication system are to be efficient. Similarly, all languages known appear to use a limited set of special address forms. Where literate societies have preserved their history, it is easy to trace back the use of forms of address, particularly in the dialogues of their plays and other literary products.

The use of the pronouns T and V

There is more than one story associated with the origin of T and V forms being used to mark something other than the simple distinction between singular and plural number. The story preferred by Brown (1965) has a satisfying appeal. After the division of the Roman Empire into two sections, the West was ruled from Rome and the East from Byzantium, thus generating political problems of preserving the two as a single unit. One small device instituted by Diocletian was that persons addressing either emperor should use the V form, since they were really speaking to both. It was simultaneously true that they were speaking to someone more powerful than themselves and through time, it was alleged, the use of V and the receipt of T became a more general sign of deference. Mutual exchange of V became a sign of equality among top people. The use of the word 'peer' has some historical similarity with such a process. An alternative argument would ascribe the use of V to powerful persons as an assumed association of plurality and power – the more there are, the more powerful they are. The Hebrew word for God was already in the plural a long time before Diocletian. The actual history is not of immediate relevance, but the story may be a welcome diversion.

Suffice it to say that mutual T and mutual V came to mark equality, emphasizing either solidarity and familiarity (T) or unfamiliarity (V), while the asymmetrical use of V to superior and T to inferior came to mark a difference in power. We shall have to examine just what these variables are, but for the moment a word like 'power' will suffice to refer to the relationship. It is possible that a single relationship will involve a conflict between the two dimensions of power and familiarity, and we can examine the factors relevant to the choice to emphasize one aspect of the relationship rather than the other. For example, within a Western European family, considerations of solidarity and familiarity would argue for mutual T among all members, but power differences between parents and children would argue for T down and V up the generations. Do children use T to parents and emphasize the solidarity or V and emphasize the deference?

In general over the past few hundred years the forces acting to abolish the asymmetric usage of T and V based on power appear to have been winning, occasionally given abrupt and dramatic expression in government edicts, as occurred during both the French and Russian revolutions. In Brown's terms the solidary semantic has been winning over the power semantic. Meanwhile the V/T distinction within its own dimension has come to have variations in domain of use in different countries. According to Brown, in France mutual T seems to be based mainly on considerations of achieved *cameraderie* rather than ascribed kinship status, while in Germany the reverse is true. The data are regrettably less hard than they might be.

From this brief discussion, we can see how a binary choice of a simple linguistic unit which can hardly be avoided in verbal interaction may be associated with much wider behavioural implications in a social relationship. The rules of any particular culture which govern this choice may be precise or vague, but the choice will in itself be informative. It appears to be related to dimensions of power and familiarity. However, before we delve a little more deeply into this, it may be fruitful to examine a feature in English address forms that continues to mark these aspects, the use of proper names.

Proper names and titles

Since the T/V distinction has disappeared from English, there are possibilities of minimizing the use of proper names and titles when addressing another person, although this possibility does not exist when we have to refer to a person absent from any on-going encounter. As the T/V distinction allowed only a binary choice, so Brown (1965) argues for the significance of a fundamental dichotomy among proper names between TLN (Title Last Name – Mr Jones) and FN (First Name – Fred), while recognizing the existence of a graduated ladder (see Figure 6).

Brown and Ford (1961) studied usage of names in a specified

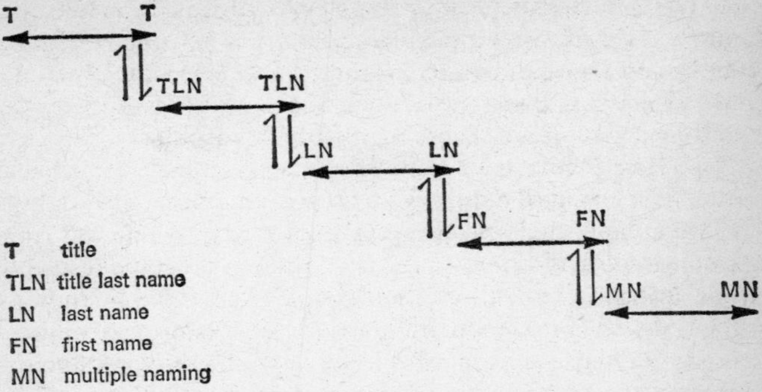

T   title
TLN   title last name
LN   last name
FN   first name
MN   multiple naming

Figure 6 Address forms for proper names in English showing common units and combinations (after Brown and Ford, 1861). Horizontal links are reciprocated forms with 'solidary' increases from left to right. Vertical links illustrate unreciprocated forms marking inequalities of power

set of modern plays, observed behaviour in a Boston business, collected reported usage by business executives and by children in the mid-west of the United States and 'Yoredale' in England. Results similar to those for V and T were obtained, and are reported in no more detail. Asymmetric usage of TLN/FN marked inequality of power. Mutual TLN marked equality but unfamiliarity, while mutual FN marked equality and familiarity. Brown notes that in a switch from mutual TLN to FN, it is the person of a higher status who generally initiates the changeover, and that this changeover can be very fast. Among present day youth in England FN can be immediate to the extent that LN may remain unknown.

Among other possibilities shown in the diagram are: title on its own (T), often an occupational rank like Colonel or Professor, but also a general 'sir' or 'madam'; last name on its own (LN) and multiple naming (MN). Brown argues for a single chain of progression: T, TLN, LN, FN, MN, citing two main reasons. First, where usage is asymmetric, this particular ladder gives the highest number of one-step differences. Secondly, where there are changes in usage with time as an index of increasing familiarity, the progression is from left to right. Subsidiary points about reversals can be made: they are associated with differential promotions in formal organizations and they can be used as mild warnings in social settings where perhaps the relationship has become more intimate than one person desires – 'Hands off please, Mr Robinson!'

To lessen the despair of those readers who have a particular reverence for hard data, and to illustrate that real life is a little more complicated and complex than might be inferred from results reported so far, it may be useful to report the results of one British investigation. Staples (1971) extended a study by Slobin *et al.* (1968) in an investigation of the forms of address used by thirty members of a large department store. She examined the address forms received and expected, four ranks of addresser, four ranks of addressee, and five variations of situation in relation to formality of address. There was a very high degree of agreement between people's judgement of what address form they would receive from whom and what others reported they would use to them. Even with non-reciprocal forms of address, 94 per cent agreement was obtained, supporting the view that these data are reliable. The addresser's rank did not of itself enable any prediction as to the form of address likely to be used, though both the situation and the addressee's rank did significantly affect the form of address. However, the *relative* status of addresser and addressee did enable such a prediction to be made. Further, both relative and absolute age of those communicating affected the form of address, young junior salesmen being relatively less formal than older people. When non-reciprocal forms of address were involved, status rather than age was more important. In a subsidiary analysis of 'disagreements', Staples found that these were confined to the three most 'informal' situations and were consistently in the direction of inferior ranks assuming greater equality than their superiors would expect. Along with other consistent results, this difference was used to formulate a general proposition that in an hierarchical organization members of inferior rank will act to minimize inequalities of status, while those of superior rank will act to maximize them, address forms being one of the pieces in the power game. The main points of this study have been published (Staples and Robinson, 1974).

In line with Hymes's (1967) ideas about relevance of situation and Labov's (1966) empirical demonstration of pronunciation shifts with changes in formality, Staples found clear evidence that 'in the store in front of a customer' was treated as more 'formal' than 'in the staff canteen', 'at a staff dance', in the street and in a pub, although 'in the staff canteen' was also significantly different from the other three. What it is about 'in the store in front of a customer' cannot be isolated. As Staples points out, the presence of the customer, the likely topics and the functions of any exchange are confounded factors.

One satisfying aspect of these investigations is that the data are such that an imaginative, thoughtful and patient detective can pursue the search for determinants – and find them more easily than is often the case.

Systematic description of the step-ladder portraying forms of address awaits further inquiry, especially at the MN end. Multiple naming is purported to be a feature of very intimate relationships, particularly that of husband and wife, in which a whole set of special names may be invented, from the common device of adding an (i) sound, Petey, to monstrosities like Robbo, Robbikins, and Gruffomorn. What would be of particular interest is the determinants of the usage of each of these forms. Married couples may have a wide variety of sub-role relationships with different divisions of labour and styles of performance, and particular forms of address may be differentially associated with these. On the other hand, they may also mark the affective state of the relationship generally. 'Gruffomorn' might be a candidate for this function. Are more highly differentiated marriages marked by a greater variety of multiple naming in line with Whorf's (1956) more general point that the lexical differentiation in a language is a function of important or frequently occurring behaviourally significant discriminations?

Questions can also be asked about the use of the last name only. My impression is that this is fairly common in formal organizations where frequent choices for two-person interactions have to be made and relatively large numbers of persons are potential candidates for these; speed of unambiguous reference may also be important, e.g. in schools, hospitals, the armed forces, etc. With thirty-five children in a class a teacher is more likely to have several Johns, Bills, Sarahs and Tracys than several Browns, Greens or even Smiths. Hence the surname is a better starting basis for unique identifications. Headmasters should also have greater problems than form-masters and hence be more likely to employ L N. But why then do girl pupils receive FN as often as they appear to? And what happens in mixed secondary schools? The use of L N alone appears to be a joint function of formality, efficiency, inequality of status, and historical tradition, but these are empirical problems still to be examined.

Meanwhile both the pronoun and proper name data provide evidence of similar determinants of usage, and it may be possible to clarify the nature of the basal communication system, whether power and familiarity are the two underlying aspects of the role relationships so signalled. We have now to decide whether these particular words are the most apt, whether the problem is dimensional or categoric, and whether the two-factor model is sufficient or not.

The power semantic

Brown shows a rare mastery of the English language and his choice of the phrase 'power semantic' has accrued to the underlying concept an attractiveness and potency which it may not fully merit. In later (and earlier) writing 'status norm' has been used.

'Status' is an unfortunate word in that in common parlance it is value-laden if not given further qualification: 'He has status' means he has a high status. In sociology, it serves as a descriptive technical term to refer to an attribute of a person or position which has general sociological significance in terms of rights and obligations, often qualified by the attribute from which the status is derived, e.g. age status, sex status or occupational status. 'Power' is similarly a technical term referring to the differential right to control another person's behaviour independently of the latter's wishes. Hence, the two terms are different in their application in sociology: power is one type of relationship which can be found between the occupiers of two or more statuses. Power is the safer term to use here, although if one is going to be very precise, it fails to cover 'authority' relationships (where rights to control are contingent upon the authority providing good reasons for following any suggestion).

As far as forms of address are concerned, the conventions already exist, and the norms governing differential usage can be given for different role relationships. Where such relationships involve differential rights and obligations which involve an imbalance of power, the asymmetric forms of address are more likely to occur. At the most general level, the asymmetry in power is expressed and reflected in asymmetry of forms of address. In our society at present these relationships are exhibited in age status differences (children–adults) and occupational status differences (boss–employee; manager–worker), both within the hierarchy of an organization and where the staff of service organizations encounter customers (madam versus miss). Incidentally it is interesting to note the difficulties involved between younger and older adults, especially where the relationship is of long standing and the gap around fifteen or more years. When the person of previously lower status is offered the right to use the Christian name of the older person there frequently appears to be a protracted period of embarrassment during which naming by the younger is avoided.

It would seem that 'power semantic' is an apt phrase to use for this differentiation in that this is the underlying relevant feature, but note that if we wish to specify the power differential between participants we need to know the pattern of rights and obligations defining their status relationship.

The solidary semantic

If we ignore the fact that this American label is less than euphonious to some English ears, there do seem to be complications with this dimension that are not involved in the other. Two strands, intimacy and solidarity, are involved. By solidarity is meant an 'us' versus 'them' division. While group solidarity may often be associated with the usage of an in-group sub-code, there is no necessary implication that the members know each other particularly well. Small combat units, ship crews or sports teams, all of which may have their primary focus on the attainment of specifiable external goals, may adopt less formal address forms emphasizing the difference between themselves and the wider society; yet their interaction may remain limited to the goals defining the reasons for the group's existence. On the other hand, increasing intimacy is also associated with a switching of address forms. A courting couple do not necessarily wish to emphasise the 'us' versus 'them' difference; they may even become oblivious to 'them' existing.

What both have in common is a fair frequency of interaction and a degree of interdependence under conditions which do not permit a stranger to enter immediately into the structure. It is noteworthy that the two aspects of this may also have different stopping points on the proper name ladder. While the groups whose cohesiveness is constrained by an external goal (or threat) may stop at LN or FN (or nicknaming), the pairings of personal intimacy are perhaps more likely to proceed to MN, in order perhaps to signal the varieties of sub-role relationship associated with a range of shared activities rather than the univariant relationship in a single shared activity.

If these arguments are valid, Brown's coinage of 'solidary' is a useful way of emphasizing the similarities between solidarity and intimacy. Both the latter terms, however, are also necessary to enable us to refer to their distinguishable features. It may prove more useful to return eventually to the use of an older term 'cohesiveness' from group dynamics, where it is used to refer to the interdependence of group members, although it was evident that this interdependence could spring from diverse sources. Such a return would be welcome if only for an integration of the knowledge derived from the study of small groups.

Evaluation of the scheme

Does the postulation of only two associated but distinguishable dimensions really serve to catch all the variance of usage? Is the problem a dimensional one at all?

One of the chronic difficulties in social science is to decide whether aspects of behaviour have dimensional or categorical characteristics. Are the underlying variables continuous like length or mass or discontinuous like ranks in the army? For example, it is argued that neuroticism is a continuous variable. We are all more or less neurotic, but for practical purposes society uses categorical judgements when it treats neurotics; some people are undergoing treatment, while others are not. In scientific theory a variable may be continuous, but technologically it is treated as discontinuous. The current dilemmas of the educational system in part arise from a need to devise a category-based system that can successfully accommodate continuous variation among children.

Forms of address are necessarily discontinuous. Where pronoun choice is available, either V or T may be used; but languages do have more finely shaded categories, as we have seen for naming in English, where there are at least five possibilities. When we switch we necessarily make a categoric shift, but there are other aspects of behaviour both verbal (e.g. forms of greeting) and non-verbal (seating patterns) which enable us to temper the extent of the shift. In other words, there is variation possible in the behaviour associated with a single form of address. For present day England, naming choices are probably best represented as a set of steps or stairs as Brown's diagram shows, although it must be remembered that they may be well-worn and rounded, by combining them with other behaviours.

At a guess, societies in which statuses are achieved make fewer precise and unambiguous discriminations and have available other options for signalling variations within a relationship in which perhaps only one basic form of address is used, whereas societies where statuses are ascribed are more likely to have a carefully graded and fine set of discriminating address forms co-occurring with other linguistic features. For example, in Javanese the address forms (and even the proper names given to people) mark a complex array of possible status relations. Not only is there a range of address forms with associated pronoun choices, but the lexical choices of some 250 person-centred nouns and verbs are associated with 'polite behaviour' terms; this marks only the starting-point of a dynamic system of considerable intricacy (Uhlenbeck, 1970).

Even within an English-speaking community we shall have to launch out beyond address form choices. Greetings and leave takings, forms of request and expression of gratitude are obvious possible sources of variation, but grammatical and lexical choices in other activities are no doubt relevant. An example of a more pervasive and dramatic special style would be the mother–child and father–child relationship (or teacher–pupil). The speech behaviour of mothers with infants is only just beginning to be investigated (Ervin-Tripp, 1971) and the evidence is presented in a form that makes earlier analyses purported to be supportive of a strong nativist view (Brown and Bellugi, 1964) even less impressive. There is some documentation of what common-sense observation might dictate, that maternal speech is telegraphic, short, simple and repetitive in structure, has a concern with such matters of immediate interest to infants as food input and output, is related to the child's understanding, and is in part dependent on the child's own verbal repertoire.

Roles in small groups

Role differentiation in laboratory constituted problem-solving groups has always been a subject of attention; after the repeated failure of the original quest for definitions of leaders in terms of traits there was a switch to a social psychological analysis of how emergent leaders differed in their behaviour from non-leaders (see Collins and Guetzkow, 1964, for a review).

Perhaps inevitably the notion of a single group leader quickly gave way to the idea of two leadership functions: the task specialist and the socio-emotional leader – the first speeding the group towards solutions of its imposed problems, the second meanwhile maintaining it as a cohesive unit. Finer discriminations can be made (Bales, 1961).

In the early phases of a group's existence it was found that task-specialist leaders talked more than other group members, especially to the group rather than to individuals, while conversely they also received more communications from other group members. Qualitative differences were described with Bales's categories: not surprisingly socio-emotional leaders emit relatively few negative reactions, but many positive ones; task specialist leaders give more information, offer more opinions and make more suggestions for action. How they do this linguistically has not been examined: the linguistic features relevant to category discriminations have been assumed rather than investigated. The fact that observers show high inter-recorder reliability, however, implies that they have the knowledge necessary to make such discriminations, and perhaps this success itself has made it unnecessary to chase the relevant structural and semantic linguistic criteria. If any socio-linguists were to divert their attention from naturalistic studies to what must now in some departments be a large store of video-recordings of small group discussions with associated Bales's categories already scored, they should be able to add to our knowledge of the linguistic realizations of these categories and expose some more precise links between role relationships and verbal behaviour, and between functions and structures of utterances.

Prescribed roles

Although prior manipulations can be effected, laboratory-located small groups often allow roles to be differentiated. In the world outside, what is prescribed in advance may be more obvious. Relationships will range from maximal to minimal discretion in role expectations and performances. The social psychologically defined relationships of 'friend', or 'hiking companion' shade off into roles intermediate in their discretion such as 'father', 'colleague', through into the highly prescribed institutionalized role performances required of persons occupying positions in the judicial, military or religious orders of society.

Although it would be unduly premature (and almost certainly wrong) to suggest that it is useful to posit a unitary dimension of amount of discretion associated with roles, amateur observation forces us to notice linguistic correlates of such a variation. In the exercise of his office as minister in church services, a priest is heavily constrained in the speech forms he can employ. In many activities he has choice only at the extra- and para-linguistic levels. Judges are not free to invent their own formulae for passing sentences, nor sergeant majors to issue personally preferred forms of orders. Newsreaders must adhere to their texts. These constraints extend through selections of alternatives, co-occurrence and sequences to render the speech forms ritualized.

Whither now?

While it may be true that all roles are probably marked linguistically, it is not clear which are worth studying and why. Applied reasons can be given, of course. For each generation being initiated into a culture, it is useful to acquire this knowledge, with a high priority to be accorded to those roles the individuals themselves will have to or will choose to play. The exposure and efficient transmission of relevant information can be justified along such lines. But at the theoretical level it is not so easy to distinguish between the trivial and the significant. How does one discriminate between intrinsically interesting case studies and exemplifications of more general principles?

Some suggestions might be made, at least in the form of vague questions. As with Labov's work on identity marking, so with role relationships. The articulation of the linguistic and non-linguistic features of a society, or any sub-culture, organization, institution or grouping within it, may well show up what is significant for that grouping. Which role relationships are marked in what ways and how obvious these are may highlight what is culturally important and what is not. The degree of differentiation and the manner of its linguistic marking along dimensions of power or cohesiveness, the priorities given when conflict of choice arises presumably mark cultural values. The extent to which something has to be said or can be left undefined may be used as an indication of how much we value individual freedom, or how much we are indifferent to social problems – both these states being able to exist at the same time. The extent to which prescriptions are found at all levels of linguistic analysis may indicate a combination of the importance of the activity to the society and a required universality.

But these grander problems may become more readily specifiable if some smaller issues are probed first. At what linguistic levels are role relationships defined? The different levels at which constraints operate might be expected to have differential significance. But as yet we know nothing about the associations between constraints at phonological, prosodic, grammatical and lexical levels. Can we find role relationships for which the constraints are at the phonological level only, and if so, what have these roles in common with each other that differentiates them from other roles?

And at a mundane practical level, can switching address forms modify the behaviour of others and if so under what circumstances and in what ways? What happens when the established norms in a relationship are deliberately flouted or people break norms of which they are unaware?

7 Regulation of Encounters and Encounters as Regulators

Regulation of encounters
Introduction

For an encounter to take place at all, there must be ways for people to signal to each other that an encounter is possible. As well as there being means of attracting attention, there must be ways of opening, maintaining and terminating the set of events comprising that encounter. The means may differ with the type of interaction. Here we shall not pursue any serious attempt to classify or even describe encounters but merely illustrate some of the ways in which verbal behaviour is associated with them – in the first section treating speech mainly as an independent variable, in the second mainly as a dependent one.

In two-person encounters involving speech, the participants will play roles of speaker and listener, and in any dialogue will alternate these. Both roles and their switching will require the exercise of what have been called social skills. Argyle (Argyle and Kendon, 1967; Argyle, 1969) has chosen the term 'skill' deliberately because these performances have sufficient similarity (or identity?) to complex sensori-motor skills, such as typing or driving, to make it well worthwhile to capitalize upon the considerable knowledge already acquired of the latter (see Annett, 1969). The pay-off has been an impressive array of findings in both the verbal and non-verbal areas (Argyle, 1969). This exploitation of a suitable model or analogy can serve not only as a stimulating heuristic device for research workers, but also as a quickly comprehensible framework for a stranger to begin to see what the problems are. To this end we may find it helpful to select a class of skilled sensori-motor behaviours having some similarity to social interaction. Ball games are an

obvious candidate, although, whereas Argyle's work emphasizes the skills of the players in working out the intentions and
behaviour of their opponents (decoding) and to a somewhat
lesser extent the skill of the players in making appropriate control movements (encoding), our interest will focus upon the
ball itself and how it gets moved about – and upon the rules of
the games themselves. In other words, instead of concentrating
upon the array of cues by which friendliness or superiority is
communicated, we shall want to know how someone knows
when it is his turn to speak; how the transition from listener to
speaker, and vice versa, is achieved – but only in so far as verbal
behaviour is relevant to these ends. Are there different rules for
different encounters? Some introductory remarks about this
possibility must be made.

Varieties of encounters

Just as there are many varieties of ball game, there are many
types of encounter, and just as no one has set out a classificatory
system of games, specifying their similarity and differences in
terms of criterial attributes, so no one has done this for encounters. One primary dimension might well be the degree of
institutionalization, i.e. the extent to which the conduct required is universal and set down in rule books. Within a game,
this can vary through time, and with place, participants,
resources, etc., at any given time. A Red Indian precursor of
lacrosse was an inter-tribal affair involving an unlimited number
of male players, almost no rules except that of scoring goals,
with a high incidence of serious physical injuries, including
deaths. At least the distance between the goal mouths and the
number of players is now restricted, even if the savagery is not.
With football the highly institutionalized league and international matches (again in some respect reminiscent of early
lacrosse?) are more closely regulated than the kick-about in a
primary school playground.

Similarly with encounters. Diachronically, judicial trials,
marriage ceremonies, or contract making and other well-
ordered social institutions, with their precise rules of procedure,
written recordings, and their backing in statute and common

law, have grown historically out of hazier, local, oral trans-
actions. Encounters which have become so institutionalized
that the regulation of events is heavily prescribed in terms of
who says what to whom when are of less immediate interest to
social psychologists than those where the rules are unwritten or
indeterminate. If one wishes to find out the rules governing
tennis or getting married, one buys a booklet or asks players
and experts already conversant with the rules. This is a more
efficient strategy than hunting for and video-taping actual
games, trying to induce the rules and making subsequent
testable predictions. Social psychologists may have an interest
in verbal behaviour involved in ritualized performance, but
they are more likely to be concerned with a focus upon the
marking of emotional states, identity, personality or role
relationships than with encounter regulation *per se*.

It will be in the regulation of sub-institutional encounters
that social psychologists are most interested. Here we may well
not be able to ask the players what the rules are; or if we can
ask, we should treat replies with scepticism. We shall be forced
to adopt observational procedures, naturalistic or experimental, formulate guesses as to what the rules are, and perhaps
finally break them in order to check the validity of our interpretations.

At present our knowledge of attention seeking and greeting
devices is confined to the anecdotal or to data collected for
other purposes. Some single units ('Hallo!', 'Charlie!') can
be made to serve simultaneously to attract attention and greet,
while in certain situations we can dispense with both and
launch straight into our message. Relationships between
participants, topic, channel and other SPEAKING factors (see
p. 34) will determine the extent to which abbreviation is
acceptable or not. This elision, in so far as it makes sense to use
this term, is not universally customary and our culture may
well be deviant in this regard. Many societies will have complex
rules of substitution, co-occurrence and sequence to be
followed in a greeting period that can last many minutes, such
that it is considered rude, uncultivated, etc., not to adhere to
these procedures. Similar rules govern leave-taking.

We have already referred briefly, while considering address forms, to the array from which selection can be made. It is suggested that 'Hi!' is less formal than 'Hallo!' or 'Good morning!', while similar assumptions might be made about 'See you!', 'Cheers', 'Farewell' and 'Good-bye'. But there are no hard data setting out the range of items, or their associated usage, or whether 'Hallo, Charlie' is used in different situations from 'Charlie, hallo!'. Who is allowed to initiate an interaction? Clearly the opening and closing phases of an encounter are associated with role relationships, and it would be absurd not to look at the two together; but apart from Schegloff's (1968) analysis of opening sequences in telephone conversations, we remain ignorant. From this unsatisfactory state of affairs, we move on to a further problem where matters have progressed slightly further.

Given that a dialogue is proceeding, how do verbal signals serve to allow people to alternate their roles as speakers and listeners? My immediate regret is that the social psychologists studying this problem have been looking, in the first instance, mainly at non-verbal signalling. From a preliminary consideration of how direction and duration of gazes were articulated with other events in two-person conversations, using a small sample of Oxford undergraduates who were asked to get to know each other, Kendon (1967, 1970) has built up a detailed picture of the synchronization of postural, gestural and other features of behaviour in face-to-face conversations. In the earlier work, functions of gaze were the predominant concern rather than speaker–listener role switching *per se*. While associations between non-verbal behaviour and role switching were demonstrated, it remains far from certain as to how significant a part shifts of gaze play in the switching itself. One of the most obvious verbal devices for switching from speaker to listener would appear to be questions, but these were not examined. To what extent an increase in the incidence of other-directed gaze accompanies linguistic (or even para- and extra-linguistic) features, but does not actually serve as a main cue for role switching, was not pursued. For switching within conversations Kendon examined whether the speaker's looking or not looking was associated with the listener's responding without a pause. An extended look from the speaker was followed by an immediate response from the listener in 70 per cent of the cases, while not looking gave pauses or failures to respond in 71 per cent of the cases. The statistical analysis given is not appropriate (calculation of χ^2 demands independence of observations, whereas Kendon sums observations across persons (1967, p. 36)), but the significance of the difference would almost certainly remain if the analysis were re-done on sound statistical premisses. This certainly strengthens Kendon's case, but it is odd that verbal content was ignored, even if it was not a main interest, and the actual analysis of non-verbal cues undertaken was in itself a mammoth task.

We do know from summaries of small-group conversations that questions have a high probability of being followed by answers, but it would be instructive to use the conflicting cue strategy of Argyle, opposing gaze behaviour and questioning, for instance, to see whether either on its own interfered with the smoothness of role switching. Argyle's conclusion that 'it is not always appreciated by linguists however that conversation would be impossible if it were not supported by non-verbal communication in a number of ways' (1971, p. 12) is premature and likely to be misleading.

What we know from Kendon's work is that a speaker is operating something akin to a symphony orchestra well scored and harmonious, but whether the average audience normally discriminates only the basic melody we had best investigate rather than assume.

There are of course two problems rather than the one presented. Not only does a listener need to know when it is his turn to speak, he needs to know when he is not expected to. Again Kendon's evidence would imply the existence of non-verbal activities concurrent with continuous speech, but it remains true that the semantic units of an utterance are broken into grammatical units and that these units may be important. For example, linguists who define a sentence as the smallest grammatical linguistic unit that can stand on its own are probably assuming that, except under conditions where various presuppositions can legitimately be made, utterances will normally consist of one or more complete sentences. People will not normally make grammatically incomplete utterances or, if they do, there may be special intonational cues of slurring accompanied by various non-verbal cues that serve as completion signals. This is an assumption rather than a fact, but if it is correct, then we would not normally expect a listener to interrupt within the bounds of a sentence. It would therefore seem sensible to include linguistic features in any analysis of cues relevant to switching and maintaining conversational roles.

It is probably appropriate to mention the filled pause in this context. Defined somewhat casually but satisfactorily as 'ahs' 'ers' and 'ums', and referred to generically as FP (filled pauses) by Maclay and Osgood (1959), these pauses were found to be in a weakly complementary distribution with unfilled pauses; they occurred mainly before lexical rather than function words. Cook's data (1971) reveal a different distribution, and show that FPs are most overrepresented just in front of pronouns. Anxiety studies have had little success in showing that filled pauses are signs of anxiety. What do they do? Maclay and Osgood have suggested that they signal to a listener that a speaker has not yet finished, but intends to continue when he has found the words. Unfortunately this reasonable idea has foundered on the rocks of hard data. Boomer (1965) argues that if this were so, filled pauses should be preceded by a longer silence than unfilled pauses, but found no empirical support for this idea: 72 per cent of FPs were not preceded by any pausing. Further, he found no differences in the location of FPs and UPs (unfilled pauses), both of which occurred most frequently after the first word in what he defined as a phonemic clause: 'hesitations . . . are most likely to occur *after* at least a pre-liminary decision has been made concerning its structure and *before* the final lexical choices have been finally made' (p. 156). This is not inconsistent with Cook's data, especially if the pronouns preceded by FPs are in grammatically complex sentences, as they may well be. The issue remains unsettled, but, although the floor apportionment retention hypothesis has received no support, a floor apportionment grabbing hypothesis remains to be investigated. Boomer found that whereas 22 per cent of FPs occurred before the first word, only 8 per cent of UPs did. Whether this would emerge as a significant difference cannot be calculated from the published data, but with 65 per cent of FPs located in either first or second position, the possibility that this is one function of FPs is worth investigating. Certainly in small-group discussions it might be argued that, given our social norms, the difficulty is to get into a conversation rather than to stay in once established.

At worst this extends the general problem in floor apportionment. As well as the pursuit of cues relevant to voluntary maintenance and relinquishment of the roles of speaker and listener, we have also to find how the roles are maintained in a competitive situation. Although initial observation might assume that competition would be primarily for the role of speaker, this would be hazardous. Where norms demand speech, successful assignment of this role to others would save a reluctant person from speaking. Kanfer *et al.* (1960) found that open-ended utterances, as opposed to interpretive ones, were associated with longer speeches from the other person. High specifity of interviewer questions was associated with low verbal productivity of respondents (Siegman and Pope, 1965). This is hardly surprising perhaps, but can we proceed to make generalizations from behaviours associated with the roles of interviewer and therapist to the idea that personality dispositions can be related to floor apportionment? For instance, do introverts and low self-revealers ask relatively more questions than extroverts and high self-revealers? Do they utilize positively reinforcing agreement signals of grunts, 'Yes's', head nods, etc., to keep the other person talking? The use of these techniques to keep a person responding has been examined, and has been extended into selective reinforcement of particular grammatical structures or lexical items with some success, under some limiting conditions (see Krasner, 1961). Conversely, disagreement signals are alleged to reduce output. While the precise associations between features of verbal behaviour and role switching, role acquisition, role avoidance and role maintenance have not been specified even at a general level, it is fairly easy to see which aspects of speech are most likely to be rewarding to integrate into the developing literature on non-verbal communication skills.

Summons–answer sequences

In a rather different vein, Schegloff (1968) has attempted to specify the sequence rules governing opening remarks in telephone conversations. From the starting point that a basic rule for conversation is that only one person speaks at a time, with an inevitable *ababab* sequence, Schegloff adds that on the telephone the answerer speaks first, giving either a straight 'Hallo!' greeting or an identification of some sort. The caller then greets and frequently identifies himself. The operation of this 'distributional rule' is followed by the operation of a further rule, 'the initiator of a contact provides the first topic'. He notes that this distribution rule can be effectively utilized by receivers of obscene phone calls: no answering 'Hallo!', no rude messages. Schegloff found the rule covered all but one of five hundred phone conversations recorded in a police station. Unwilling to treat a single caller's initiating 'Hallo!' simply as a deviant case, he suggested that the issue be generalized into a study of summons–answer sequences. Reviewing his analysis, Schegloff presents the following exchange:

SUMMONER Bill? (A summons item; obligates other to answer under penalty of being found absent, insane, insolent, condescending, etc. Moreover, by virtue of orientation to properties of answer items, i.e., their character as questions, provides for user's future obligation to answer, and thereby to have another turn to talk. Thus, preliminary or prefatory character, establishing and ensuring availability of other to interact.)

SUMMONED What? (Answers summons, thereby establishing availability to interact further. Ensures there will be further interaction by employing a question item, which demands further talk or activity by summoner.) (p. 1091).

Those of more cynical and impatient disposition may query the utility of this microscopic examination. Certainly there is a prima facie case to be answered as to what ulterior purpose might underlie this measure of meticulousness. Baldwin's maxim of 'Wait and see' may be an inconclusive injunction, but until such approaches as Schegloff's can be shown to have classificatory or heuristic possibilities, this may be the best policy. Recalling our earlier mention of Aristotle's stipulations about definitions, and derivatively, descriptions as well, the successful analysis of summons–answer sequences can only take on theoretical significance when contrasted with other types of sequences in terms of similarities and differences. Hopefully some categorization along these lines may emerge, but we may note in passing that telephone procedure is more like tennis than a sub-institutional activity in some respects. Children may well be taught explicitly to give name and/or number when answering a call, and to ask who is calling whom: the telephone directory explicitly mentions identifying oneself as a sensible strategy for the receivers of calls. Rules can be and have been formulated about efficient ways to proceed with this means of communication. Rules for radio transmission are even more explicit. One wonders therefore whether deviation from these rules constitutes anything more than a failure to learn them?

Whither now?

Some priorities for research can be asserted without reservation. The first would be a development of the work on role switching but including linguistic analyses of the verbal behaviour. We need to know which of the many possible cues available are used for smooth dialogue and discussion within a limited range of encounters. We know something about the non-verbal possibilities and could quickly integrate these into investigations in such ways as to determine which cues are relevant to not only role switching, but role acquisition, maintenance and avoidance as well. While we might expect variation with the SPEAKING variables, sound descriptions within limited contexts should quickly reveal how the relevance of particular features shifts – hopefully explanations of such shifts would also begin to emerge. A more adventurous undertaking, unlikely to commend itself to anyone who is not obsessional, would be to try to build up a classificatory scheme for encounters.

Encounters as regulators

Introduction

While the verbal behaviour of one person can act as an independent variable affecting the structure of an encounter,
influences in the other direction and in interdependent relationships are easily derived from Hymes's mnemonic. Changing
settings, participants, ends, message form, topic and instrumentalities can all modify verbal behaviour. Moscovici (1967)
reviews some contrasting studies of the effects of ends; brief
mention will be made here of spatial arrangements, channels,
topic and participants.

Spatial constraints

Mehrabian and Diamond (1971) – with an experimental design
not immune to criticism – illustrate how closeness of seating
and orientation of speakers are associated with the amount of
conversation ensuing; Sommer (1969) had previously emphasized the relevance of seating positions to role relationships and
their associated linguistic correlates. While he did not argue the
priority of role or verbal behaviour, earlier work on restricted
channels of communication in small problem-solving groups
clearly showed their interdependence (Bavelas, 1950; Leavitt,
1951). Change the communication channels and, other things
being equal, patterns of interaction and role relationships
change. Manipulate role relationships and the patterns of
interaction change.

Channel constraints

By 'channels' we mean the media in which messages are transmitted from emitter to receiver. Verbal messages can be
received as written and therefore visual, or as oral and therefore
auditory input. But a letter differs from a conversation in other
ways. Extra- and para-linguistic cues are reduced, at least in the
minds of those who have no faith in graphology. It is more
likely perhaps that the wilder unsubstantiated claims of handwriting character-readers have led to the possibilities of handwriting as a source of information about personality being
over neglected. (Handwriting is as much a form of expressive

behaviour as some others which are accredited greater respectability.) Further, natural conversations can allow the situational, postural and gestural cues to have full play, whereas variety in letters is reduced to types of paper, class of mail and some other seemingly insignificant sources of variation.

On the basis of previously established grammatical and lexical differences between speech and writing, Moscovici (1967) devised a number of oral situations which restricted communication in ways similar in some respects to those associated with writing. Discussing films and the cinema for twenty minutes, pairs of subjects were assigned to one of four conditions: face-to-face, back-to-back, side-by-side, or face-to-face but with a screen blocking their vision. It was predicted that sitting back-to-back or side-by-side with no head-turning would be sufficiently unfamiliar to subjects, but involve constraints similar to writing, for speech under these circumstances to contain a higher proportion of nouns and connectives and fewer verbs than the face-to-face conditions. Moscovici pleads for the similarity of the two face-to-face conditions, 'the elimination of purely gesticulative or mimic elements from a communication channel is not enough to cause modification of syntactic organization' (1967, p. 258). Results were as predicted. What would be interesting to know is whether the differences would be maintained if subjects practised at length under these and other conditions. What other linguistic features might change, and what non-verbal changes occur? We have not as yet even compared telephone and face-to-face conversations where it would be easy to control for participants, and topic with experienced telephoners, familiar with the channel constraint. The results for the condition using the screen are puzzling.

Participants

Two separable theoretical issues are necessarily linked in natural situations – personality and role relationship; we expect role relationships to constrain verbal behaviour, but personality characteristics also affect what is said. Earlier chapters have indicated some of the cues that receivers or observers use to assess or identify attributes of persons or relationships. However, these investigations were not generalized; we did not ask about the extent to which emitters can or do vary their speech as a function of whom they are talking with.

One hypothesis offered is that response matching is likely to occur at those linguistic and even paralinguistic levels that are compatible with other contextual constraints. This reservation is necessary because the situation may demand complementary rather than similar behaviour from participants. A teacher's questions may be more likely to evoke answers from pupils rather than further questions. An interviewer's questions are unlikely to be reciprocated. On the other hand, Giles (1972) has demonstrated a convergence of accents between participants, while Jaffe and Feldstein (1970) showed pause duration of speakers varying with participants' pausing behaviour. More generally, Jourard (1971) argues for reciprocated increases in self-disclosure. One of the more dramatic exemplifications of this will be parent–child interaction. Some students of children's speech (McNeill, 1970) in part based their beliefs about the development of grammatical competence upon the strange assumption that the speech of a mother to her child followed adult rules. The empirical absurdity of such beliefs is now beginning to be demonstrated in data showing considerable structural and lexical similarity between the speech of mother and child (see Ervin-Tripp, 1971).

This adaptation of mothers to the capacities of their children is one instance of a further issue about the extent to which speakers are able to adapt their verbal behaviour to special attributes or limitations in their listener. Flavell and his co-workers have looked at this problem developmentally and have shown increases in role-taking proficiency with increasing age, for example, in talking to a blind or a younger listener (Flavell, 1968). Creed (1972) showed that undergraduates required to communicate to a fellow student and a ten-year-old child reduced the total amount of information transmitted, cut down on complex structures, longer words and lexical diversity for the latter. Interestingly enough, in an unpublished pilot study, Creed found that a sample of teachers overestimated the abilities of children of given ages to use items from the vocabulary sub-scale of the WISC by a wide margin. One of the alleged characteristics of the speech of the lower working class is that it fails to take into account the possible ignorance or different perspectives of listeners (see chapters 8 and 9).

Topic

While it is obvious that the incidence of particular words will differ from topic to topic however we classify topics, it is not obvious that the general linguistic structure will change as we switch our focus from flowers to fish. That the form of relationship existing between topic and participant affects verbal behaviour has been shown in a series of experiments by Creed (1972). Moscovici (1967) had shown that 'familiarity' of participants with a topic was associated with high lexical diversity of speech. Creed varied both 'familiarity' and 'involvement' in tasks where each person had simply to find out information from another person. In general, high familiarity and involvement were associated with diversity of lexis and a relatively high incidence of pronouns, but a number of indices of grammatical structure showed no sensitivity to the experimental manipulations.

Whither now?

To build up a systematized framework for describing and explaining encounters as regulators is going to be difficult. The isolated investigations mentioned link up selected features of verbal and non-verbal behaviour. One can envisage a strategy in which a systematic variation of all values of the SPEAKING factors, singly and in increasingly compounded interaction, is pursued. But to link up all the verbal and non-verbal features in such a fashion does not commend itself as a feasible project. At present we are almost reduced to a Baconian position in which we might engage in several 'I wonder if . . .' investigations, trusting that a persistent gazing at the results will eventually lead to a useful theoretical insight. On the linguistic side, we have access to detailed descriptive systems at levels of analysis from phonemics to syntax. The relative weakness in semantics and pragmatics may encourage a neglect of these aspects, but hopefully not. On the non-verbal side our descriptive capacities for talking about types and forms of organization and institutions are probably sufficient for us to specify relationships between the linguistic and non-linguistic worlds. We do not as yet have any higher order explanatory framework to link the two, however.

At the sub-institutional level we can describe and explain behaviour in limited settings, but the emphasis in social psychology has been placed on studying process rather than content. Group dynamics has excited more enthusiasm than a taxonomy of groups; processes of role differentiation have been paid more attention than listings of roles. It was mentioned in chapter 2 that the study of structure without function is as fruitless as the study of function without structure, but the articulation of the two can only be achieved for sets of behaviour where the same rules apply. If different rules apply in different sets then the absence of such controls will generate only confused and confusing results. This is readily illustrated earlier in this chapter. If people can hold 'successful' telephone conversations, it necessarily follows that roles are maintained with a total reliance on cues coming in on the auditory channel. The visual reception of the other person's eye movements and gestures cannot be relevant cues. Hence, without prejudice as to how things work in other situations or how they are learned, if roles can be exchanged satisfactorily on telephone links, visual cues are not a necessary condition for achieving this. Anybody who mixed up telephone and face-to-face conversations in his collection of data might extract some higher order propositions about dyadic interaction, but he would miss the difference between telephonic and face-to-face situations. Hence, we need to specify the relevant variables and classify interactions in terms of the values they have on these. Hymes's SPEAKING poses the problem, but it is the specification of the significant variables covered by each letter that is required next.

8 Social Class and Language

Introduction

Why treat social class as a variable that merits special consideration in a general review of relationships between language and social behaviour? A weak reason is that there is empirical work to report about the subject. Like Mount Everest, it is there. Better reasons can be given. The majority of problems and studies mentioned so far have been of a social psychological nature, concerned as they are with functions and patterns of speech in face-to-face interaction: how encounters are regulated, role relationships expressed or defined, how individuals do or can draw inferences about the states and conditions of others. These and other problems can also be investigated at a sociological level of analysis (or of course a social anthropological level). It seems appropriate to include at least one area of study at a level beyond social psychology, at the same time illustrating how the two disciplines are connected.

It is also true that work already mentioned has concentrated upon descriptions and explanations of the performance of adults: we have not asked how people come to learn what they know. In fact, since we know little about this as yet, the omission is unavoidable. By contrast we can adopt a developmental perspective with social class and language, this policy having a double advantage. To describe and explain the developmental processes has an intrinsic value; it also helps to exemplify the relation between sociology and social psychology. For example, the sociological specification that life chances differ according to differences in starting position defined by social class may be partly explicated when one begins to examine the differences between the child-rearing practices of L W C and M C mothers.

This is an example of how the sociological is translated into the social psychological. Chapter 9 concentrates upon socialization, while this chapter attends to social class differences in language behaviour *per se*.

We must briefly mention problems of the definition of social class. Sociologists have not been as helpful as they should have been. On the one hand, there are philosophical theories of class with definitions based on the differential distributions of power over a variety of environmental features; on the other, classes are defined pragmatically by measurable indices of income or prestige. The links between the two are not immediately obvious. The operational indices themselves are varied. The seven basic category scale of Hall and Jones (1950) is derived from the prestige status of occupations as judged by a sample of the adult population of Great Britain. The four category A–D system preferred by market research organizations is based on income and patterns of consumption. The Registrar General's 1961 Census (General Register Office, 1960) used five social class groupings, but these can be contracted down to manual or non-manual or expanded into seventeen or more socio-economic groups. The categories and their ordering are derived presumably from the judgements of experts who have taken into account income, prestige, type and degree of skill, length of training, as well as rural/urban distinctions. In fact, indices of occupational prestige, income, amount and quality of education, place and type of domicile are highly correlated (see, for example, Brandis, 1970). It is as well to remember that, given this complexity, it may be an improper question to ask to what social class a person belongs when the normally associated criteria are found to diverge. It may also be more useful to use one index than another in particular inquiries. For example, if we were interested in what the patterns of beer consumption were likely to be, the occupation of husband might be more useful than education of wife. However, the gap remains between such indices and a Marxist or Weberian analysis of class, and neither is likely to be of immediate use if we are interested in family life styles, for instance. In fact, investigations making comparisons most frequently rely on the

indices most easily obtained and are not really concerned with
higher level theories of social stratification. Unfortunately this
can lead to a misleading degree of over-simplification. Bernstein's analysis provides a case in point. When writing about the
working class and codes of language use, he has insisted that he
is contrasting the *lower working class* (semi-skilled and unskilled) with the middle class, yet in writing about his ideas,
other people frequently drop the term *lower*. This can make a
substantial difference.[3]

But are there social class differences in language use and if so
what are they, what do they mean and why should they occur?

Fries and Schatzman and Strauss

A truly scholarly approach to the problem of social class
differences in language use and usage would require us to trace
a long history of anecdotes, observations and ideas. Such an
enterprise is well beyond the present frame of reference, but
there are two studies conducted before the 1960s that are worth
more than a brief mention. Fries (1940), in an almost totally
neglected book, set out to specify grammatical differences in
letters written by professional and lower class correspondents.
Schatzman and Strauss (1955) successfully anticipated many of
the semantic and pragmatic features of lower working class
speech, later mentioned by Bernstein, in the analysis they made
of interviewees' accounts of a tornado in Arkansas. Both
investigations are of methodological interest in that they
exemplify in different ways investigations at the initial stages of
scientific inquiry.

Fries is explicit about his criteria of social class, except in one
respect. To be in the working class group, the respondents had
to have left school before ninth grade (basic secondary); certain
formal non-linguistic features of the letters had to indicate more
than semi-literacy (spelling, capitalization and punctuation);
and their occupations had to be 'manual and unskilled',
paying them less than ninety dollars a month. The tag 'manual

3. Where investigators have clearly used lower working class subjects,
LWC is used; where it is either ambiguous or skilled workers have been
included, WC is used.

and unskilled' is ambiguous. The sample was also biased to the extent that those LWC persons who were illiterate or semi-literate were excluded directly – or of course did not even write in. Three hundred such letters were used; the number of 'professional' letters is not mentioned. Here, the criteria for inclusion amounted to three years college education, membership of a generally recognized profession and non-linguistic literacy. Following these descriptions, the elaborate analyses of these samples of 'vulgar' and 'standard' English are then presented as total counts or percentages. No statistical analyses were conducted, nor are they possible on the data as given. Strictly speaking, no reliable inferences about differential usage can be made, in spite of a meticulous attention to the provision of information about the scoring of the linguistic categories. Schatzman and Strauss, on the other hand, offer little information about procedure, no description of scoring, no descriptive or analytic statistics, but plunge quite happily into statements about the social class differences 'found'. What is even more irritating is that, having broken one of the more binding rules of the scientific game – that the steps between hypotheses and conclusions should be publicly available – they come up with results that later workers have arrived at only after rigorous and painstaking adherence to the rules.

While some later studies of social class differences in language use have unfortunately not taken the linguistic notion of register into account, both these investigations did. Precise information is lacking, but Fries's letters were all apparently sent to an administrative department of the armed forces that dealt with exemptions from service, payments to dependents, compassionate leave, etc. Hence there was an experimental control for topic, and possibly for problem within topic, i.e. letters were generally requests for action backed up with supporting arguments (a personal inference from the examples!). They were all formal in that the recipient was an unknown bureaucrat and, of course, they were written rather than spoken. Similarly, all the speech analysed by Schatzman and Strauss had been orally related to an unknown interviewer who might be assumed to be unfamiliar with the events which were to be described, and this speech was also about a single topic – the tornado.

With slight hesitation a number of results are offered in Table 3 as a summary of Fries's data. They represent a number of morphological and lexical differences that would probably have emerged as significant if they had been properly analysed. Syntactic differences also occurred.

Table 3 **Some morphological and lexical differences between standard and vulgar English** (from Fries, 1940)

More common in standard		*More common in vulgar*
Nominal group		
Head:	plural zero form	s-less form for time and distance when deviant
Modifier:	nouns, double	–
Intensifier:	more, most	-er, -est
	suffix -ly	all, awful, bad, but, mighty, pretty, real, right
Pronouns		
Plural form:	–	youse, you all, you people
Verbs		
Lexis:	–	get, do as full verbs
Modals:	should, might	would, can
Tense:	have+been+past participle	has been
Prepositions		
Location:	–	with pronouns
Lexis:	by, during, of, until, upon, with, within	for, about, at, under, without, till, off, onto, double prepositions (off from)
Function Words		
Lexis:	that, which, while, who	and, but, as, if

What can be extracted? WC letters differ from MC letters in several respects that might reasonably be attributed to dialect; the WC usage of 'My son James, he . . .' does not result in ambiguity or indefiniteness. On the other hand, their more frequent usage of the verbs 'do' and 'get' suggests a preference for leaving information less precise than it might be, while the more frequent usage by M C writers of certain prepositions and compound nominal groups may signify a greater concern on their part for precision. There seems to be a greater concern to make meanings unambiguous and organized.

Although the validity of their categorizations is not that obvious, Schatzman and Strauss report their results under four headings: perspective, correspondence of imagery in speaker and listener, classifications used, and framework and style of ordering in the description.

W C speakers are reported as retailing events from their own perspective only. They did not accommodate to the fact that the listener had not been present. 'We', 'they' and persons' names were used with no explicit reference or further identification. There was no qualification or elaboration, and phrases such as 'and stuff like that' were substituted for more detailed exposition. Information given was concrete, referring to particular individuals rather than to roles, groups or organizations. Finally, stories were basically straight narratives, but digressive, one observation triggering off a second, which triggered a third sometimes unconnected with the first, except by verbal devices such as 'and', 'then' and 'so'. The authors employ the analogy of a cine-camera moving around from place to place with the speech being a loose commentary predicated upon the assumption that the listener is watching the same film.

By contrast, the M C accounts shifted perspective from self, to other individuals, groups or organizations; the listener was supplied with context to set the stage for events to be related; possible disbelief and misunderstanding were anticipated; and meanings were qualified to take into account the listener's absence from the events. Classifications transcended the particular and attempted to order the total action. The narratives themselves were tightly organized with considerable cohesion, digressions occurring but only as sub-plots followed by a return to the main theme.

The results are explained in terms of life styles and the likely needs of the speakers to relay information. It is suggested that the W C speaker normally deals with 'listeners with whom he shares a great deal of experience and symbolism' where 'motives are implicit and terminal requiring neither elaboration nor explanation' (Schatzman and Strauss, 1955, p. 337). The authors did not notice the possibilities of comparison with Piaget's work showing that children take their own point of view prior to realizing that other people have different ones, that they learn as they grow older to handle longer and longer sequences, and can handle the particular before the general, the concrete before the abstract. One suspects that investigators are loath to infer that some sub-cultures of a society may be more child-like than others.

These two studies contrast in one further important way. While Schatzman and Strauss ignore grammar and lexis, except where they can use such units as indices of one of the categories in which they are interested, Fries meticulously sweats through the grammatical indices with no obvious concern for the significance that these might have in communication situations. While Fries is all structure and unit, Schatzman and Strauss are implicitly function orientated. The difficulty is to integrate the two.

Bernstein

A hiatus of several years was followed by Bernstein's entry into the field from a different tack. Why do L W C children not do better in the educational system? Almost any index of 'better' will suffice to show up social class differences, from entry into higher education to attainment within stream of school. Bernstein (1958) argues that a major neglected determinant of these differences is likely to reside in a differential use of language: the lower working class use language mainly to define role relationships (public), whereas the middle class use language for other functions as well (formal). He later listed likely structural characteristics of 'public' and 'formal' languages (see Table 4) in an attempt to integrate the functional codes and their structural realizations. The subsequent evolution of these ideas is charted by Lawton (1968).

Table 4 **Characteristics of public and formal languages**
(after Bernstein, 1961, p. 169)

Public language
1. Short, grammatically simple, often unfinished sentences with a poor syntactical form stressing the active voice
2. Simple and repetitive use of conjunctions (so, then, because)
3. Little use of subordinate clauses to break down the initial categories of the dominant subject
4. Inability to hold a formal subject through a speech sequence; thus, a dislocated informational content is facilitated
5. Rigid and limited use of adjectives and adverbs
6. Infrequent use of impersonal pronouns as subjects of conditional clauses
7. Frequent use of statements where the reason and conclusion are confounded to produce a categoric statement
8. A large number of statements/phrases which signal a requirement for the previous speech sequence to be reinforced: 'Wouldn't it? You see? You know?', etc. This process is termed 'sympathetic circularity'
9. Individual selection from a group of idiomatic phrases or sequences will frequently occur
10. The individual qualification is implicit in the sentence organization: it is a language of implicit meaning

Formal language
1. Accurate grammatical order and syntax regulate what is said
2. Logical modifications and stress are mediated through a grammatically complex sentence construction, especially through the use of a range of conjunctions and subordinate clauses
3. Frequent use of prepositions which indicate logical relationships as well as prepositions which indicate temporal and spatial contiguity
4. Frequent use of the personal pronoun 'I'
5. A discriminative selection from a range of adjectives and adverbs
6. Individual qualification is verbally mediated through the structure and relationships within and between sentences
7. Expressive symbolism discriminates between meanings within speech sequences rather than reinforcing dominant words or phrases, or accompanying the sequence in a diffuse, generalized manner

Table 4 — *continued*

8. It is a language use which points to the possibilities inherent
in a complex conceptual hierarchy for the organizing of
experience

A small misunderstanding?

Subsequent empirical work has generally been directed towards
the establishment of the facts about grammatical, lexical,
semantic and pragmatic features distinguishing L W C and M C
usage, but while the results have been confirmatory, it is still
possible to raise certain criticisms. One type of attack at least
needs a short digressive comment. About the Bernstein work,
Labov has written:

There is little connection between the general statements made and
the quantitative data offered on the use of language. It is said that
middle class speakers show more verbal planning, more abstract
arguments, more objective viewpoint, show more logical connections, and so on. But one does not uncover the logical complexity
of a body of speech by counting the number of subordinate clauses.
The cognitive style of a speaker has no fixed relation to the number of
unusual adjectives or conjunctions that he uses. . . . When we can
say *what* is being done with a sentence, then we will be able to
observe how often speakers do it (1970, p. 84).

Coulthard has suggested that code differences are simply
quantitative,

The figures [Bernstein, 1962b] suggest that the linguistic performance
of the working class boys, as a group, is depressed in relation to that
of the middle class boys; they certainly do not show two distinct
groups 'differently oriented in their structural selections' (1969,
p. 45).

If we concede that Labov's stricture about the lack of connection between the theoretical statements made and the
predicted linguistic differences has a measure of validity, and
that the *logical* force of his later remarks has power, this does
not prevent us from posing questions about the significance of
the quantitative differences found. Labov argues that 'when
we can say *what* is being done with a sentence, then we will be
able to observe how often speakers do it' (1970, p. 84), but is it

not also the case that if we observe how often speakers use certain forms in certain contexts, we may be able to hazard some guesses as to what they are doing with their sentences?

Similarly Coulthard's worry may carry logical force, but be empirically empty. Take for example the set of objects labelled 'ships and boats'. Are the differences among them quantitative or qualitative? We could use a fleet of coracles as platforms from which to throw stones at an offending galleon, but a suitably equipped twentieth-century guided missile delivering destroyer would solve the problem with greater ease. Ships differ in function, and within economic and engineering limits their structures are related to these functions. Particular ships can be refitted or adapted to improve their efficiency or change their use. To use certain basic similarities as an argument for potential equivalence in other ways or as an argument for ease of conversion would not impress a marine engineer who was asked to run up an aircraft carrier out of a Roman galley. If we were to take this large set of objects labelled 'ships and boats', group its members into sub-sets, and then count or measure the structural variables, only quantitative differences could be found – by defined parameters of the investigation. As with one technological innovation, so with another. Given that we analyse two sets of speech corpuses in terms of a *single list* of linguistic categories, we can only arrive at quantitative differences, even if certain categories have a null entry in one set. Both Labov and Coulthard are making a fairly deep error. Similarities and differences can always be found between any sets of elements, and these can be expressed quantitatively. This logical point does not have significance *in vacuo*, but might have in particular cases. We may, however, pause to sympathize with the possibility that Labov and Coulthard are posing a serious objection, namely, that we cannot argue from a set of quantitative differences *back* to a qualitative distinction. What they have failed to see is that this was not the direction of the original argument – which was from function to structure. While Bernstein's argument takes the form 'If A, then B' and the data show up features relevant to B, all empirical science has this characteristic.

A similar problem arises with differences in the use of lexical items. Bernstein states:

The restriction on the use of adjectives, uncommon adjectives, uncommon adverbs, the simplicity of the verbal form, and the low proportion of subordinations supports the thesis that the working class subjects relative to the middle class do not explicate intent verbally (1962b, p. 234).

That lexical differences occur, and these have been reported with fair frequency (Bernstein, 1962b; Lawton, 1968; Robinson, 1965b), indicates something and is probably not irrelevant. Bernstein's argument is that the code differences are likely to result in lexical differences, although the existence of these differences does not necessarily imply differences in code.

Bernstein's theoretical framework

There are a number of difficulties associated with an exposition of Bernstein's theoretical framework, and it may be helpful to distinguish some of the distinguishable levels of analysis.

As a *sociologist*, Bernstein is concerned to specify sociological conditions conducive to the development of different communication systems. He has chosen to focus attention on the differences in the positions and life styles of the lower working class and the middle class in twentieth-century Britain – a complex urban industrialized society with a class structure that allows some mobility. His observations obviously have a potential relevance both to other class and caste-based societies. Retaining a sociological perspective, Bernstein is also interested to explain how 'special' forms of communication are retained from generation to generation, especially in the circumstances prevailing in Britain where the existence of a universally available primary and secondary education might be expected to remove such differences. An analysis of these sociological problems might well enable a specification of language codes which are likely to maintain a *status quo*. As one example, we should expect that the codes of the under-privileged groups would not facilitate the verbal expression of an accurate analysis of their situation – working class consciousness may require a command of an elaborated code of language use before the condition can be articulated and communicated.

One common idea in the background of many explanations is the 'least effort' principle: organisms are not likely to proliferate and develop many capacities beyond their needs. The work roles of low social status groups currently and previously have involved relatively unskilled repetitive tasks. Verbal instruction will not have been particularly significant for the learning of the skills (see chapter 3) and verbal interaction on a job that involves no more than brief commands or requests will not be necessary (and conditions of noise, etc., may well discourage anything more than the brief exchanges of repartee). Neither subsistence farming nor unskilled factory work require great mastery over the referential function of language and the associated structures and lexis.

As Bernstein writes more generally:

If a social group, by virtue of its class relation, that is, as a result of its communal function and social status, has developed strong communal bonds; if the work relations of this group offer little variety; little exercise in decision making; if assertion, if it is to be successful, must be a collective rather than an individual act; if the work task requires physical manipulation and control rather than symbolic organization and control; if the diminished authority of the man at work is transformed into an authority of power at home; if the home is over-crowded and limits the variety of situations it can offer; if the children socialize each other in an environment offering little intellectual stimuli; if all these attributes are found in one setting, then it is plausible to assume that such a social setting will generate a particular form of communication which will shape the intellectual social and affective orientation of the children.

Such a code will emphasize verbally the communal rather than the individual, the concrete rather than the abstract, substance rather than the elaboration of processes, the here and now rather than the exploration of motives and intentions, and positional rather than personalized forms of social control (1970, p. 28).

While this list has persuasive appeal, it does not yet have the orderliness that will eventually be required. Eventually it will be necessary to disentangle those attributes of low social status that are functionally related to particular codes and those which are incidental to these. It will be necessary to investigate which attributes of class are determinants of code, which consequences and which are interdependent. This last form of relationship is one which sometimes presents conceptual difficulty for people who hold beliefs based on only a simple cause/effect model. 'Does A cause B or B cause A?' can be an improper question in several respects. First, it presupposes that a single variable analysis can be applied rather than a complex interactional one. Secondly, it presupposes a single direction of causation rather than a two-way relationship; and thirdly, it confers a discreteness upon that event rather than viewing it for example as a (dis)continuously operating servo-mechanism. The class/language code problem is probably best construed as a servo-mechanism – with negative feed-back loops. The lower working class status and particular language codes are locked together. Any potential change in role definition is constrained by conceptual categories linked to a code of language usage. Any potential change in conceptual categories and associated verbal representation is constrained by role definitions. If this is so, we may have to rest content with an explication of the facts of life style and language use – and point out how they mesh. To ask how they came to fit is to ask historical questions. To begin to answer why they continue to do so from generation to generation is taken up in the next chapter. And this will involve a shift from sociology to social psychology and to psychology, and back again.

It is not difficult to see how certain aspects of life style will relate to language use. If the work situation requires no speech, either in learning or execution of the work task, there is no need for a learner or operator to have a language available for this. Many unskilled, semi-skilled and even skilled jobs come close to this. If the work situation requires fast, unambiguous verbal instructions to be decoded, a specialized and efficient jargon is likely to develop, as in aircraft control, deck behaviour on yachts, trawlers or warships. If the work situation involves a heavy proportion of reception, transmission and production of verbally encoded information (as in bureaucratic positions), only minor adaptations to the forms of everyday general language code may be necessary. For specialized activities in the law or science, distinguishable and different language codes are necessary. There will also be demands in bureaucratic, business and scientific posts for a considerable degree of correspondence between what is said or written and the non-verbal world, that is, a premium will be placed on effective use of the referential function. Crudely speaking, one can see what type of relationships are likely to exist between work and use of language.

It is not so likely perhaps that leisure pursuits of brass bands or bingo rather than Bach or badminton will be functions of language codes. We shall then need some much closer specification of those aspects of lower working class life style that are causally linked to language usage and those which can be attributed to other factors such as tradition, aesthetic preference or lack of material resources.

In the meantime it may be useful to offer a summary of some of the empirical evidence obtained. Features particularly associated with language development and socialization are treated separately in chapter 9. Here a brief review of other differences is given. This is complicated by the fact that the subjects of investigation differ in age from young children to near adults. It might have been appropriate to present results systematically separating phonology, grammar, lexis, semantics and pragmatics for encoding and decoding of both speech and writing, if the primary interest had been linguistic. In time it may be possible to start at the pragmatic end and show how differences at that level are realized semantically, how they are achieved by a differential use of grammar and lexis. At present this can not be done. Studies are reported by author, with an attempt at a final interpretation. This gives rise to some confusion. Some workers have collected speech, some writing, while others have used the written medium for collecting information about speech. Conditions of collection vary from free discussions to controlled filling in of gaps in sentences and identifying grammatical roles of nonsense words. Studies have varied in the levels of linguistic analysis attempted. The order of presentation is as far as possible: grammar and lexis within speech, then in writing and in mixtures, followed by semantic and pragmatic studies.

Empirical evidence
Speech

While Schatzman and Strauss (1955) and Fries (1940) cited their undocumented differences at various levels of linguistic analysis with no controls for possible differences in intelligence, both Bernstein (1962a, 1962b) and Lawton (1968) controlled for verbal and/or non-verbal intelligence test scores. Using tape recordings of small group discussions about the abolition of capital punishment by sixteen-year-old boys, Bernstein (1962a) found that LWC subjects used a longer mean phrase length, a shorter word length and spent less time pausing than MC subjects. In line with Goldman-Eisler's (1968) interpretation of pauses as indications of verbal planning time, Bernstein argued that LWC subjects were spending less time planning because the sequences they were producing were heavily precoded 'chunks' and hence highly predictable for the speaker. These same oral materials were subsequently analysed for grammatical, lexical and other differences. Extent of subordination and complexity of verb stem (including passives) were greater in MC speech. 'I' was more common in MC speech, but 'you' and 'they' less so. Lexically, 'uncommon' adjectives (and all adjectives), adverbs and conjunctions were less frequent in LWC speech. Sociocentric sequences such as 'wouldn't it?', 'isn't it?', and 'you know', were more frequently used by LWC, and 'I think' was more frequently used by MC speakers.

Lawton (1968) repeated Bernstein's design, increasing the standardization of the procedure and using more generally accepted linguistic indices. He also included twelve-year-olds in the investigation. Very similar results were obtained with sociocentric sequences and the use of 'I think', structural complexity with the verb group, personal pronouns, and the range of adjectives and adverbs used, especially with the fifteen-year-old boys. The way in which use of subordinate clauses is related to class is shown up by Lawton's employment of the Loban Index (Loban, 1963, p. 6) which measures the 'depth' of a clause. Using this index he found that the deeper the clause, the greater the social class differences. Lawton also examined the semantic quality of utterances, with a four-fold distinction between (i) abstract, (ii) category (class of events), (iii) concrete, and (iv) clichés and anecdotes. Abstract arguments and categorial examples were more common in M C speech, concrete and particular examples in L W C speech. This was true in both age groups. Anecdotes and clichés did not give a significant discrimination, although younger boys were more likely to use them.

Similar differences were found with the fifteen-year-old boys in individual interviews where subjects were required to narrate a story about a series of pictures, describe features of their previous school, say what they thought about the purposes of education, say what they thought a 'good' teacher would be like, and justify commonly accepted solutions to some moral problems (Lawton, 1968). Lawton additionally examined whether there were shifts in style from description to abstraction. Nine indices, of which all were grammatical except the ratio of egocentric to sociocentric sequences, showed shifts in a consistent direction overall. Twelve-year-old M C subjects shifted more than L W C subjects on all nine measures, fifteen-year-old M C boys showed a greater shift on seven. Interestingly enough, Lawton did not find significant differences in a content analysis of the moral judgement answers. His conclusion was:

... in an 'open' situation the working class boys tend to move towards concrete narrative/descriptive language, but in a structured situation where they have little or no choice about making an abstract response, they will respond to the demand made upon them. They may have found the task extremely difficult, but it was not impossible for them (Lawton, 1968, p. 138).

Not impossible perhaps, but the examples of their performance offered by Lawton (1968, pp. 134–8) show little systematic organization.

Evidence for differential tendencies to switch styles has also been put forward by Henderson (1970b) for five-year-old children. MC children changed the proportions of form classes used more than LWC children as task demands switched from description to narration. As part of the same study, she found considerable differences in type/token ratios for adjectives and nouns, with MC children being higher. With a related sample of children, Hawkins (1969) found that LWC in narrative stories and descriptions were less likely to specify referents of pronouns (this, that, here and there). They also used fewer epithets at head, fewer modifiers other than 'big' or 'little', fewer ordinatives, intensifiers or rank-shifted clauses at head. In both cases, however, materials discussed were visible to both child and interviewer.

Two recent failures to find class differences in the United States have unfortunately to be written off for methodological reasons. Shriner and Miner (1968) found no differences in the ability of young children to apply certain morphological rules to nonsense syllables; but although their two social class groups were matched on age and Peabody Picture Vocabulary Test scores, these were on mean scores only. The age range was two-and-a-quarter years, and since age was a relevant source of variance, a matched-pairs design at least would have been necessary to provide a sensible test. LaCivita, Kean and Yamamoto (1966) also reported no class differences in the use of morphological and syntactic cues to identify parts of speech; but since their analysis was in fact by school and the MC schools had only 58 per cent MC pupils and the WC school 76 per cent WC pupils, their conclusion is hardly warranted. Both studies have been reported (Cazden, 1970) as though they provide evidence relevant to the issues of the relationship between language and social class.

Using elicited imitations of sentences involving six instances of verb inflexions, three in MC and three in their LWC forms, Jordan (1972) found no differences with nursery school children in their ability to imitate, but both groups showed strong tendencies to change presented forms to those appropriate to their class norm. While this is clear evidence for grammatical differences in use at an early age, the investigation seems to pose the further problem that *both* groups must have been able to *recognize* the form from the other social class in order to make the appropriate changes.

Writing

Lawton's (1968) results with four essays the boys wrote and with the sentence completion tasks they performed yielded similar grammatical, lexical and semantic differences to those found in speech. The semantic features examined were two estimates of the proportion of abstract and general content in essays on 'Home' and 'My life in ten years' time', both having a higher incidence of occurrence in the writings of older and middle class boys – and within the range of the sample, class was more relevant than the age gap. This contrast is illustrated with two examples:

Working class fifteen-year-old boy's essay on

My life in ten years' time

I hope to be a carpenter just about married and like to live in a modern house and do a ton on the Sidcup by-pass with a motor-bike and also drinking in the Local pub.

My hobby will be breeding dogs and spare time running a pet shop. And I will be wearing the latest styles of clothes.

I hope my in ten years time will be a happy life without a worry and I have a good blance behide me. I am going to have a gay and happy life. I am going to work hard to get somewhere in the world.

One thing I will not do in my life is to bring disgrace and unhappiness to my family (in Lawton, 1968, p. 112).

Middle class fifteen-year-old boy's essay on

My life in ten years' time

As I look around me and see the wonders of modern science and all the fantastic new developments I feel a slight feeling of despondency. This is because I am beginning to wonder who will be in control of the world in ten years time, the machine or man. Already men are being shot around earth in rockets and already machines are being built that will travel faster and faster than the one before. I wonder if the world will be a gigantic nut-house by the time I'm ten years older. We are told we will be driving supersonic cars at fantastic speeds, with televisions, beds, and even automatic driving controls. Do we want this, do we want to be ruled by machinery. Gone will be the time when the family go out for a picnic on a

Sunday Afternoon, we will be whisked along wide flat autoroads we will press a button in a way and out will come a plate of sandwiches ready prepared. You may think that this is a bit far fetched but if things keep on improving men will not have to think for themselves and we will become a race of bos-eyed mawrons. There is, if this is going to happen, no way to stop it. Men say we will have just one or two more luxuries and it never stops. I enjoy the luxuries of today, but in my opinion there is a limit. But who decides what the limit will be. No one knows its just a lot of men all relaying on someone to stop this happening, but non-one is going to. We're doomed. No prayers can save us now, we'll become slaves to great walking monstrosities. Powerless in the hands of something we helped to create. I'm worried about 'my life in ten years time' (in Lawton, 1968, p. 113).

Lawton points out that the differences found can be said to reflect only choice and not capacity, but this is a hypothesis that can be tested.

For twelve-year-old children writing informal and formal letters, Robinson (1965b) found significant social class differences, mainly in the informal letters for both boys and girls. The formal letter was to be addressed to a school governor explaining why the child should be given a prize to go on a visit or holiday. The informal letter was to a friend sick in hospital describing what had been going on in the last fortnight. Grammatical differences, apart from errors, were few in number and not systematically consistent with Lawton's results or Bernstein's theory. Lexical differences in the informal letters were consistent with both. There is some worry that the working class in this investigation were not purely lower working class, a fair proportion being children of fathers in skilled manual occupations. In addition, the grammatical indices were not linguistically respectable.

Cloze procedure

Cloze procedure is a technique devised by Taylor (1953) in which a corpus of speech or writing has artificially created deletions made in it and subjects have to guess what has been omitted. Successful decoders (gap fillers) are presumably familiar with the language habits of the encoders. By varying encoders, decoders, messages and types of deletions, a range of possible questions can be posed. In this context we can ask about the ways in which WC and MC decoders fill in gaps created in speech and writing of WC and MC encoders.

Robinson (1965a) collected sentences obtained from the samples of the speech and writing of thirteen-year-old WC and MC boys and deleted one item (noun, adjective, verb, adverb, preposition, pronoun, conjunction) from each. MC and WC subjects, controlled for verbal and non-verbal intelligence test scores and a measure of vocabulary in use, were required to write in words that might fit in the gap in the order in which they thought of them. For twenty-five out of thirty items MC boys gave a wider variety of responses than WC boys. The most common word chosen by one social class group was unlikely to be the most common response of the other. Finally, measures of conformity were calculated for each item. The most common first response of WC boys was used by more of them than the most common response of MC boys. A measure which took into account the frequency of occurrence of all first response words also gave differences between the groups. The greater conformity – and hence predictability – of WC responses was confined to the written items. Unfortunately this type of approach has not been developed, either in terms of giving oral presentations with oral replies or in terms of using a greater variety of language samples to see to what extent members of different classes are better at predicting gaps from speech of their social peers.

Deutsch, Levinson, Brown and Peisach (Deutsch *et al.*, 1967; Peisach, 1965) explored the relations of age, sex, intelligence test scores, race and social class to filling gaps created in both teacher and child speech. They used criteria of correctness of responses rather than conformity – correctness defined absolutely, contextually (semantic sense preserved), and grammatically (in term of form class). For teacher speech, the superior performance of MC children was eliminated when statistical controls for intelligence test scores were introduced. For eleven- to twelve-year-old children's speech, the more efficient guessing of MC children survived partialling out of intelligence test scores. While MC and WC children were equally effective at guessing gaps in WC speech, MC children were more efficient than WC children on MC speech. Similar results were obtained with race, Negroes having relatively more difficulty than whites with the speech of white children, rather than vice versa. The investigators used auditory as well as visual presentation in their design.

Williams and Wood (1970) deleted every fifth word from four-person group discussion sessions involving MC and WC Negro junior high school girls talking about students' problems and attitudes to school. A research student attempted to manipulate the style of the discussion by adopting standard English for a formal discussion and what is referred to as 'home-talk' for an informal one. MC girls were more efficient than WC girls at prediction overall, this being particularly true for predicting MC speech. It was true of absolute and form class measures, and for omissions of both lexical and function words. The omissions from WC speech were more accurately filled than those from MC speech. However, the manipulation of formal and informal was not very successful. WC girls apparently switched styles more than MC girls, although what this means cannot be inferred from the journal article since the authors confine themselves to noting, that '... WC encoders were markedly reticent in the formal condition'.

These three studies give a consistent picture of the greater redundancy of WC speech and writing for both MC and WC decoders, but the attempts to vary the other scales of register (mode, style and topic) have not given useful information. There are clearly opportunities for manipulating these aspects, as well as participants.

At least two technical difficulties need to be overcome. Robinson's decision to use written presentation of oral utterances can be criticized on the grounds that it would be more appropriate to use oral administration. However, Deutsch *et al.* (1967) report much lower scores with oral presentation, arguing that this technique places a heavy memory load on the subjects. With first-grade children they were forced to delete the last words of sentences to make the administration feasible. It might be instructive to contrast the two methods empirically with comparable samples of subjects.

A second difficulty consists in the decisions as to what are to constitute 'correct' answers. Taylor (1953), Deutsch *et al.* (1967), and Williams and Wood (1970) all used the deleted word as a criterion of correctness. Robinson argued that this could be construed as only one response for that location and that degree of agreement among subjects was of more relevance for estimates of predictability. While this argument has some merit, high agreement on the part of WC children as to what a teacher has said when they are all wrong is clearly not satisfactory. The dilemma may be a false one. Each calculation may have a utility contingent upon the purpose of the investigation.

Relationships between function and structure

The structural and lexical differences so far mentioned are most likely to have semantic and pragmatic significance. The LWC use of a less complex grammar, a less diversified lexis, and the relative lack of change in proportions of various structures and items as the task definitions are changed suggest a lack of adaptability with changing circumstances – a lower degree of efficiency of communication, if by efficiency we mean unambiguous reception by a mythical generalized listener or reader with a minimum of effort. But such summary statements are by no means inconsistent with Labov's criticisms which, although couched in terms of the misleading quantitative/qualitative issue, also raised the question of what people are doing with the utterances they make.

If we accept Bernstein's original thesis that the restricted code of the lower working class is primarily geared to direct control of behaviour and role definition in face-to-face situations, are the empirical studies cited strictly relevant to this? Or are they more relevant to demonstrating that when the language used is geared to the referential function, LWC respondents are less efficient than MC ones? In fact, in all the studies reported, the referential function was of prime significance as far as the task requirements were defined. In many, the communication was to be received by a MC person, e.g.

Lawton's interviews and essays, Robinson's letters to a school governor, Fries's letters to government officials, Schatzman and Strauss's interviewers. In some studies the written medium was used. But is the L W C restricted code ever in written form in its natural state? It is, of course, quite appropriate to examine the adequacy of the language used to transmit meanings in such settings and report structural and lexical indicators of difference that may be relevant to probable sources of inefficiency. But even this has only been done at a general level. Schatzman and Strauss write about failures to organize material or to take the ignorance and possible different imagery of the listener into account, but they do not instantiate with any precision how these failures are realized structurally and lexically. The other studies report these differences, but tend not to show how they relate to failures in efficiency of communication. Generally the lesser syntactical complexity and narrower lexis of L W C subjects more than suggest a lesser capacity for the efficient transmission of a variety of referential messages. Even with the indicators of sympathetic circularity, there is no independent evidence brought forward to show that these are social psychological checks upon agreement – a reasonable hypothesis but needing stronger evidence in the long run.

There are a few investigations that have tried to relate structure to function in situations where the referential use of language has been at a premium. Rackstraw and Robinson (1967) looked at answers of five-year-old children to questions about how a toy elephant worked, what titles they would suggest for some pictures and how 'Hide and Seek' is played. The speech of M C children was both more general and more precise and displayed more signs of an objective rather than a self-centred perspective. These attributes were exemplified in their lexical choices, grammatical constructions and use of pronouns, i.e. the differences in communicative efficiency can be exposed by a linguistic analysis.

Explicitly dissatisfied with the idea of the pursuit of grammatical and lexical differences exemplified by the Bernstein, Lawton and Robinson studies, Williams and Naremore (1969) have contrasted functions of speech used by some 200 ten- to thirteen-year-old children interviewed about three topics: games played, TV, and vocational aspirations. Adopting extensions and giving operational definitions to some of the features of speech examined by Schatzman and Strauss (1955), Williams and Naremore found a number of class differences: LWC speech contained a higher proportion of incomplete sentences (fragments), and LWC replies to initial questions were more likely to be minimally acceptable simple responses without elaboration. This was mainly in response to questions about TV, where the LWC replies to 'Do you watch TV?' were often a plain 'Yes!'; MC children were often more prone to begin mentioning programmes and their contents. When the LWC children were pressed to elaborate, these class differences disappeared. For perspective, they found LWC more likely to use a generalized 'You' in describing the game (previously found with five-year-olds by Rackstraw and Robinson, 1967) but otherwise a self-singular stance was preferred. This contrasted with the MC third person perspective. MC answers were more highly organized, while LWC children were more likely to use request interjections (e.g. What do you want?) and phrases of sympathetic circularity. This work begins to tie up structures with function in a limited set of situations.

But is there a more positive side? What is it that the LWC do with language? Do they write less? When they write letters, to whom do they write and for what purposes? What linguistic features characterize their letters? What are the functions and structures used in telephone conversations? Similar questions might be asked about the role of speech in everyday situations at work and home. We have no observational studies that begin to answer these questions. How much role definition and direct control of behaviour is there. And what about other functions and their associated linguistic features? Are the rules governing the forms of speech in encounter regulations peculiar to a subculture? What are the rules relevant to affective instrumental activities? Clearly the opportunities for research work in these areas are many, and we have hardly begun to make even naturalistic observations of the ethnography of communication and the relevance of language to this. Such activities have not been prosecuted with any social group for any comparative purpose as yet.

By way of consolation we can begin to see the emergence of a pattern in social class differences in mother–child interaction and the studies reported in the next chapter do begin to show what LWC mothers do, as well as what they do not do.

9 Social Class, Language and Socialization

Introduction

The agglomeration of social class differences in child-rearing beliefs, attitudes and practices enforce the use of some selective principle here, even though our interest is already confined to the development of verbal skills only. While we might properly be concerned about each of the four activities of speaking, listening, reading and writing at all levels of linguistic analysis and could cover development from birth to maturity, we shall not. If we assert that essentially what we wish to know here is whether or not we can establish a *prima facie* case for the existence of functional differences in the use of language, with the lower working class emphasizing direct control of behaviour and role definition, we can answer this most readily by making a mainly patriotic survey of the work of Bernstein and his colleagues.

We could start with the presumption of social class differences in interactions of mothers with their children along the theoretical lines suggested. It is their behaviour that we would expect most generally to be relevant to what young children acquire, purely on the basis of time spent together. The simplest principle of transmission would claim that the children's learning is a direct and simple function of what is made available for them to learn. The actual mechanisms might be specified in terms of Skinnerian and/or Piagetian concepts. What the children learn will guide their behaviour.

In the other direction, the mother's behaviour will be determined by a combination of her knowledge, beliefs, attitudes and relevant constraints in the total context: one would expect her 'ideal strategies' to be modified by such constraints, whether these be acute, e.g. very busy and tired, or chronic, e.g. seven children in the family. The attitudes of the mother herself have no direct relevance to the child's behaviour for they are at two stages removed from it. More distal still, the mother's basic capacities and dispositions will be related back to social class. Why members of particular social classes should have the capacities and dispositions they do is a sociological and historical problem.

These different features of the problems are mentioned here because some odd thinking can result if the distinctions are not preserved between what used to be called immediate and final causes on the one hand and between social psychology and sociology on the other. Social class of mother does not cause children to answer questions in peculiar ways, mother's beliefs that children should answer interviewers' questions does not cause them to do so. As we have already mentioned, this type of mistake is not discouraged by the design of the many investigations that do directly relate mother's social class to child's behaviour in terms of the statistical analyses conducted. The intermediary links are often assumed rather than made explicit.

In what follows three levels are separated out: mothers' attitudes; mothers' actual and reported behaviour; children's behaviour. All of these are related back to social class. The interrelationships of the three are not explored both because it is social class which is of direct relevance to the theoretical framework and because so few studies have tried to descend to social psychology for both sets of the variables believed to be related.

Mothers' attitudes towards language and language development

Henderson (1970a) analysed data relevant to mothers' reported frequency of speaking for each of a listed variety of reasons. A set of items labelled 'social chit chat' did not differentiate between MC and LWC mothers, but LWC mothers claimed to speak more often than MC mothers for affective (e.g. to show my feelings to others) and role defining (e.g. to decide what is right and wrong) reasons, while the reverse was true for what were labelled cognitive reasons (e.g. to exchange ideas).

These preliminary results pose the problem of how far even self-report inventories might shed light on what people do with language.

More directly related to child-rearing, Bernstein and Henderson (1969) asked mothers how much more difficult it would be for a dumb mother to teach her child a number of things. Items were grouped into 'general cognitive', 'affective' and 'specific skills'. M C mothers saw greatest difficulties overall, but this was particularly pronounced in the general cognitive area. L W C mothers reported that the teaching of specific skills like learning to dress would be most affected and emphasized difficulties in this area more than M C mothers. (Work on complex sensori-motor skills in fact stresses the desirability of actual practice with knowledge of results for efficient learning of these.) M C mothers also expressed a readiness to talk with their children across a wider variety of situations and a greater willingness to answer difficult questions than L W C mothers (Bernstein and Brandis, 1970).

Mothers' beliefs about language development in children, how they think it comes about, and what relevance they consider their own behaviour has for this remain unknown. From more general evidence, it might well be expected that M C mothers believe that children have to be taught how to speak and that it is part of their role to encourage such development in a systematic way. As we shall see below they also use language as a means of communicating information of a referential nature. On the other hand, L W C mothers are probably more likely to adopt a passive view believing that children learn to speak 'naturally' or 'automatically'. This *laissez faire* policy is supplemented by beliefs in boundaries being maintained between school and home – teachers teach children school topics and the mother teaches the child role-appropriate behaviour. These possibilities have not been systematically examined.

Reported behaviour of mothers

Cook–Gumperz (1973) has analysed mothers' responses to questions about controlling their child's behaviour, namely, discipline problems. A distinction was made between 'imperative techniques', 'positional appeals' and 'personal appeals'. *Imperative* techniques included brief commands such as 'Shut up!' as well as non-verbal intervention like smacking and forcible removal from situations. Of the other two verbally based strategies, *positional appeals* comprised those reasons given for behaviour in which membership of a general status category was invoked, often age, sex, or family, e.g. 'Only little boys pull their sister's hair!' What are given here are prescriptions for behaviour appropriate to a given role, e.g. 'five-year-old boys'. By contrast, *personal appeals* invoke the consequences, affective and/or behavioural, for specified individuals such as self, mother, sister, e.g. 'Now you've broken that cup and I am very angry. You will not take advice. You have to learn the hard way, upsetting everybody'. These appeals tend to combine specificity and generality, specific acts being related to general consequences for specific people. There is also in the example an implicit higher level principle 'You should not make people angry.'

There were no social class differences in the incidence of positional appeals, but MC mothers used more personal appeals specifying consequences for the child than LWC mothers, while the exact reverse was true for imperative techniques. Comparable results have been obtained with slightly younger children in Nottingham (Newson and Newson, 1970) and with Negro children in Chicago (Hess and Shipman, 1965).

What do these results imply? In the first place LWC mothers are less likely to use language in discipline situations except in the form of direct commands. Their greater use of simple commands or non-verbal strategies leaves the child to work out for himself the connections between other events and the maternal intervention. On a classical conditioning paradigm, avoidance learning, mediated or not by anxiety, should associate contiguous events with the maternal behaviour, e.g. looking at the clock, day-dreaming about sweets, as well as spilt tea. Repeated trials with consistent reinforcement should render the learning more specific to 'offences', but the other associations might well remain unextinguished. On cognitive developmental theory, the child should seek to accommodate such experiences and derive working rules to apply to them, but the representation of this knowledge at five is likely to be mainly enactive and ikonic, neither of which permit higher order abstraction. There is the further possibility that maternal interventions are not perceptibly rule-following with sufficient consistency for successful accommodation to be possible. Newson and Newson (1970) remark upon the relatively high incidence of threats used by W C mothers, often involving outside authority figures such as policemen. Since policemen seldom come in to carry out maternal threats Newson and Newson ask how far such tactics encourage both a fear and ultimately a contempt (at the impotency) of authorities.

Given that the child can learn the positional appeals, these do afford definitions of role-appropriate behaviour. Where the appeal is based on sex or age relation, such rules have potential durability, but where they are based on age they do not. A caricature might offer a picture of a child spending his sixth birthday checking which rules for five-year-olds continue to apply – and perhaps sadly finding that many still do. It may also be noted that positional appeals define only a small number of roles and that these are ascribed and hence inescapable.

Personal appeals have rather different possibilities as opportunities for learning. They are in fact used to make referential statements about the material and social environment. Emotional states are defined verbally, and actions leading to their occurrence specified; they are made specific to individuals, hence allowing that differences between persons may exist. But children may also acquire information about more general social matters: where one buys teacups to replace broken ones; that lemon juice removes tea stains from tablecloths. It has already been mentioned that such appeals often invoke rather general moral principles, like not hurting other people. Such principles give explanations for behaviour – whereas positional appeals only assert what is allowed or proper – and hence the child has the opportunity of applying them to new situations. He can pose problems in terms of who will be hurt. 'I give you a new commandment: love one another . . .' is used to transcend eight of the Ten Commandments. Cook also found that MC mothers were more likely to take the child's intention into account, and we may note in passing that this is referring to an unobservable variable less easily inferred than emotional states.

To summarize briefly, LWC children are exposed either to conditions similar to those that a rat in a maze enjoys when learning to avoid electric shocks, or to prescriptions for role-appropriate behaviour. Language is used as a medium for the direct control of behaviour by commands or to define roles. MC children also receive such prescriptions, but in addition are given verbally expressed reasons for certain behaviours and information about the material and social environment in general. For the LWC child to contest the validity of a positional appeal or an imperative is to challenge the authority of the mother. A MC child can question the empirical basis of personal appeals without necessarily evoking such a confrontation.

Robinson and Rackstraw (1967) analysed answers that mothers said they would give to a variety of 'wh' questions supposedly posed by their five-year-old children. In this situation MC mothers were more likely to answer the questions, gave more factual information when they did, the information was more accurate and the types of explanations to 'why' questions differed. MC mothers were more likely than LWC mothers to mention causes, consequences, analogies, and class (not social for once) membership as reasons; LWC mothers were more likely than MC mothers to answer by re-organizing the question as a statement – 'Because they do', or by making an appeal simply to the regularity of the event – 'They always do'. These LWC replies make it tempting to argue that, as in the discipline situations, LWC mothers are more prone than MC mothers to control the child directly than to extend his general knowledge. Rackstraw (Robinson and Rackstraw, 1972, p. 244) argues for a grouping of certain types of reply to 'why' questions which she calls answers that 'focus on the proposition'. To use these a person need have no empirical knowledge relevant to the question, but only a small set of sentence frames, e.g. '. . . always . . .'. What are called appeals to essence, denials of a need for an explanation, and appeals to unspecified authority or tradition for moral and social questions are combined with repetitions of questions as statements and appeals to simple regularity to form the total set. In a subsequent analysis of similar data, Robinson (1973) found LWC mothers used 'focus on proposition' modes of reply more often than MC mothers. This study also found that MC mothers were more likely than LWC mothers to use more than one mode of explanation and more likely to point to similarities and differences in their answers.

What is made available for children to learn in this situation? The fact that LWC children are more likely to receive no answers or to receive only 'focus on proposition' modes to 'why' questions might be expected to discourage them from asking questions. Curiosity is neither satisfied nor encouraged. LWC children are receiving less information of a referential nature and what they do receive is less accurate. The relative absence of analogies, or specifications of similarities and differences, or appeals to categorization for 'why' questions reduces the chances of knowledge becoming organized – co-ordinate, super-ordinate and sub-ordinate groupings are less likely to develop. The relative shortage of appeals to cause and consequence reduces the extent to which knowledge acquired is ordered sequentially and meaningfully. Language is the medium by which these differences are made explicit.

A methodological critique

It might be argued that what mothers report does not relate in any systematic way to what they in fact do. Perhaps LWC mothers are nervous talking to interviewers, and this anxiety affects their verbal behaviour in interviews. If this were so we might expect to find a higher refusal rate among the working class, in what was after all a voluntary situation, and we might expect to detect some of the signs of anxiety mentioned in chapter 4. The first was not true. The second was not systematically investigated, but superficial impressions of the tape recordings do not support this idea. Alternatively, MC mothers may be operating under the influence of a 'social desirability' response set, the tendency to give some type of ideal rather than true answers (Edwards, 1957). Investigations into social desirability as a factor influencing replies normally exploit overtly obvious statements of opinion to which it is relatively easy to distort replies, whereas in this investigation no easy opportunities for distortion were available; mothers had to construct their replies from their own resources and had no foreknowledge of how their answers were likely to be scored. It is possible that the maternal replies provided would not in fact be employed with their children; especially perhaps when domestic situations become fraught with many simultaneous demands, informative causal answers to 'Why are you so red in the face, Mummy?' may not have a high frequency of occurrence. On the other hand, when moods are good and pressing problems few, we might reasonably expect MC mothers to offer more. One way of looking at the problem would be to suggest that, while almost all mothers may well use non-verbal means of control and not reply to questions under some conditions, some mothers are less likely to start in this way under favourable conditions, conditions describable in terms of numbers, types and strength of pressures to do other things.

While these worries about the validity of maternal reports should be exposed and their force investigated, it is also possible to check what the children are like. If the children's behaviour relates to the maternal reports, and we can generate reasonable explanations for such associations, the likely validity of these reports is enhanced.

Behaviour of children

Robinson and Rackstraw (1972) interviewed fifty-six children whose mothers' answers had been collected two years earlier. These children answered some of the same questions as their mothers, but the number of questions was made up to thirty, covering the full range of common interrogative words as well as different content areas for 'why' questions. In reply to these, MC children gave more information, the information was more accurate and their answers were less likely to be irrelevant to the question asked. For 'when' and 'where' questions, distinctions of convenience were made between absolute (e.g. on 17 October 1941) and relative (e.g. when my sister got married; when the bell goes) answers. In contexts where absolute answers were more likely to be useful, MC children gave more of them. In answer to 'why' questions LWC children used more appeals to simple regularity (e.g. always) and unspecified authority (e.g. it's naughty), while MC children made more appeals to classification, cause and consequence, more to wants of individuals, and mentioned effects upon other people more often. Among appeals to consequence, LWC children were more likely to mention avoidance of punishment as a reason for not doing things, the reality-based wisdom of this being complemented by Cook's data.

The parallels between the social class differences of both mothers and children have been developed in an extended re-analysis of these data in mother–child pairs within social class (Robinson, 1972). Although the sample size was small and there had been a two year gap between the collection of mothers' and children's answers, in which children had been exposed to the influence of their schools, mother–child similarities could still be found – although some strange findings emerged as well. The simplest interpretation remains: that the learning opportunities offered by the mother are determinants of the verbal behaviours of the children.

Turner (1973) has also used the factorial sample of five-year-old children whose mothers were included in the Robinson and Rackstraw study (1972), as well as a sub-sample of the same children at seven, for an analysis of control directed speech. These children had to tell a story to a series of questions asked about a four picture cartoon strip in which some boys appear to kick a football through a window, and subsequently interact with a man and possibly with a woman as well. In summary, he found that LWC children were more likely to cite tellings off and use abrupt imperative commands and context-specific threats, while MC children were more likely to use positional appeals focused upon the affective state of the controller. MC children made more explicit reference to attributes of offenders and the effects on controllers; used intensifiers (e.g. very) to make more specific reference to states; and they offered fewer examples of implicit reference marked by exophoric pronouns.

As with the question-answering, so with the control situation: if we make allowance for the difference in level of cognitive development between mothers and their five-year-old children, the social class differences among the children echo their mothers.

Observed mother–child interaction in a teaching situation

Hess has conducted a series of investigations examining relationships between maternal attitudes and behaviour and children's cognitive development. Of immediate interest are those studies which show social class differences in maternal control procedures and in maternal teaching styles (Hess and Shipman, 1965). With Negro mothers of four social class groups equivalent to upper middle ($n=40$), upper working ($n=42$), lower working ($n=40$), and a fatherless public assistance group ($n=41$), they found control differences similar to those reported by Cook (1971). The categorizations of control were different in that non-verbal strategies and positional appeals were combined into an imperative–normative category, but personal appeals were divided into those with an affective basis and those with a cognitive–rational one. The results were like Cook's. Social class differences appeared on all three categories in the expected directions. These results are mentioned not so much to demonstrate cross-cultural similarities, but to suggest that Hess's subsequent results on maternal teaching styles and children's behaviour are likely to have been found with the London sample as well.

As a warm-up task a preliminary teaching problem was set to each mother with her four-year-old child as pupil. This was followed by a block-sorting problem requiring simultaneous categorization on two attributes (each two valued). The mother was given as long as she wanted to teach her child and was told to continue until she was satisfied with her child's performance on the task. The child was then tested both for the accuracy of his performance and for his ability to verbalize the basis of his sorting. The mother–child interaction was recorded. The higher social class children made more correct sortings and verbalized these more accurately, although no co-variance analysis appears to have been used to ascertain whether the more effective verbalizations were not simply a direct function of having more correct solutions to verbalize. In their teaching, M C mothers were more likely to seek to motivate the child, establish an appropriate set, give positive verbal reinforcement, give specific instructions and seek verbal responses from their children. They were less likely to give negative verbal reinforcement or seek non-verbal feedback, i.e. to get the child to move the blocks around.

The second task, Etch-A-Sketch, utilized a commercial toy which consists of a rectangular white screen with two control knobs that can be turned to produce black vertical and horizontal lines respectively. The toy was explained to the mother and it seems to have been established that she knew how to work it effectively. The child was brought into the situation and the instructions given: the mother was told she was to operate one knob, the child the other; she could say or do anything except actually turn the child's knob (or his hand on the knob), and after three minute's practice, they were to copy five patterns. The interaction was observed, tape-recorded and accuracy scores computed. The three-minute practice session was rated for preciseness and specificity of instructions given; a sample of twenty-five instructions in the test session was scored for specificity of instructions; and a count was made of the number of designs to be copied shown to the child. A combination of these scores gave a multiple correlation of 0·64 with a measure of task performance. The class differences were considerable; the middle class performed better, but spent less time on the task. M C mothers gave more specific instructions and showed their children more of the designs and were rated more highly in the practice sessions. Some of the differences were extraordinary. The 'highest' level of instruction given by any working class mother was 'Turn your knob'. The mean number of designs shown to working class children by their mothers was only 1·2 out of the five possible.

Hess and Shipman summarize the position of the working class child in this situation:

The lack of meaning in the communication system between mother and child is clearly exemplified in the behavior of many of the mothers on this task. Consider the plight of the child whose mother is low on these three measures (see above): during the practice period, his mother demands that he turn his knob, but she fails to explain why or to relate it to the lines on the screen. During the task she doesn't show him the models and fails to give specific turning directions. For such children, the effects are these: (a) the child is not given a goal to make his individual responses meaningful (that is, he is not shown the model). (b) The mother is not specific in her directions: each new response is essentially a guess. (c) The sequence and pattern of response is not explained. The child has no way to tell ahead of time how to respond, and even after he does respond, he cannot predict the mother's reaction. He is hindered in learning anything from one response that will generalize to the next. (d) Nevertheless, his responses are being rewarded or punished, usually with maternal praise or disapproval, which provided belated feedback for a particular response if the mother is not giving specific directions. In either case, reward or punishment performs a motivating function.

As a result of the interaction of these factors, the child is being made to produce responses that from his point of view are not related to any visible goal, are unrewarding in themselves, and do not bring corrective feedback that will enable him to avoid punishment.

Nevertheless, reinforcement continues, and punishments are usually more frequent and intense than rewards (1967, p. 79).

Discussion

The data on socialization procedures are generally much more informative about functions of language and social class than the earlier work focusing mainly directly upon grammar or lexis. A number of the studies mentioned are able to relate functions and their structural realizations, particularly that of Turner. This is presumably a direction that should lead to progress. A detailed list of functionally based modes of control can be defined in terms of linguistic structure and lexis. Hence the function of 'controlling behaviour of others' can be subdivided into a variety of means and these can be cross-referenced to other functions. Abrupt commands are one form of control, but might involve some affective instrumental component. Positional and personal appeals involve role definition, the former in terms of crude status-based categories, the latter at a most general level of how human beings should behave. The personal appeals can also be linked to the affective instrumental and to the referential functions. The successful production of articulations of function and structure in limited contexts should help to lessen the force of Labov's stricture that Bernstein's theoretical framework has gaps between the two.

While the investigations reported throw light on the mother–child interaction situation, especially at the social class level of analysis, these are at least two obvious next steps. One is the shift to a social psychological analysis within or independent of class and one or two studies have begun to explore this. The other is to examine teacher–child interaction in the schools. Unpublished data from Bernstein's team on this topic may well turn out to show a correspondence between teachers' and mothers' control strategies, teachers in solidly working class schools tending to use working class strategies, those in solidly middle class schools, a middle class pattern. Demonstrations of such differences would further substantiate Bernstein's thesis. If LWC children, already orientated towards the use of language for direct control and role definition, find their teachers biased in the same way, then what has been said about encouraging and discouraging development along Piagetian lines in the home may be continued into the educational system. At present we do not know whether or not this is the case.

If it is, then it would add further support to Bernstein's explanations of how the restricted code of language usage and its consequences for the development of intellectual maturity are transmitted from one generation to the next. It has been suggested that the family and peer group will act to confuse the child, while his own cognitive-motivational predispositions and the school will facilitate his intellectual development. If it does emerge that the school joins parental and peers' pressures, then it is the child alone who is wishing to insist that the emperor is naked.

In the course of the previous nine chapters we have raised many more questions than we have answered, but hopefully we can at least begin to see some profitable directions for further inquiry at the levels of both details of investigations and theoretical objectives. As we have moved from function to function, there have been shifts in the type of linguistic features upon which attention has been focused. For emotional states, extralinguistic, paralinguistic and prosodic features are prominent. For the marking of social identity, that combination of acoustic properties enveloped by the term 'accent' and the pronunciation of particular phonemes have attracted most investigation; for role relationships, the differential use of specific lexical address forms. Structural features are mentioned briefly for performative and aesthetic functions, but only come through with some vigour in the social class studies. In those particularly, it is possible to contrast functions and begin to show how the use of particular units and structures relates to them. Furthermore, a case can be made out for the relative weakness of the referential function and its structural realization among members of one subculture. We have been able to illustrate how such a code might be transmitted from parents to children.

For some linguists and psychologists, the referential function of language has a peculiarly attractive appeal, and they may feel that the early chapters, with their emphasis on units rather than patterns of verbal behaviour, have not been concerned with the unique features of language, especially when that emphasis has been on features of speech that hardly merit mention in most standard textbooks on linguistics – the paralinguistic and prosodic. It was suggested in chapter 1 that the preoccupation of many linguists with grammar, specifiable in terms of the morphology and syntax of phonemes and units composed from these, while of considerable value in itself, nevertheless underplays the significance of other features of language which, to a naïve observer, would seem to merit inclusion. It can be asserted, however, that patterns of stress and intonation are best treated as essential rather than peripheral features of the language. In English, 'He is the man you are looking for!' might have any one of several meanings until accorded markers of stress and intonation. If Chomsky's comment that the essence of a language system resides in the relationships achieved between patterns of sound and patterns of meanings is true, then the definition of 'sound' should not be restricted to units composed only of vowels and consonants, but should be widened to include the total range. Just as the vocalic patterns of speech production are an integral part of any utterance, so are the semantic characteristics of the units and patterns employed. The apparent ambiguities of sentences, whose surface structures are apparently identical, do not necessarily require an analysis of deep structure and an application of transformational rules to reveal their differences. An analysis of the meanings of the words themselves can frequently provide the required clarifying criteria.

This is not to deny either the legitimacy or the significance of the transformational approach. It is also thoroughly commendable to push such ideas to the limits, in order to see just what they might be able to account for, but it should be remembered that there are levels of analysis other than the narrowly defined one of syntax recently espoused. The point made in chapter 1, that the language system functions by employing units which can be linked to form patterns by means of certain rules of combination, is worth repeating. Patterns so framed may function as *units* for the next level of analysis. A word, then, is a structure; it is a compound one, made up of both a combination of phonemes and, when produced, a combination of prosodic features as well. It also functions as a unit in the structure known as a sentence, which again is compounded through the application of syntactic, prosodic and semantic rules to its constituent elements. To concentrate on syntactic rules for the formation of sentences out of words is to omit much. We ought also to remember that the ultimate goal of transformational grammar is a chimera (see below).

The recommendation is that, in the study of the intersection of language and social behaviour, we should be pleased to use the insights of transformational generative grammar and remember the possibly unique qualities of our language system, but we should not be over-dazzled by this approach. We should maintain an extended view of the nature of language and include aspects of non-verbal (including vocalic) as well as verbal behaviour within our initial frame of reference. We might reasonably be concerned to examine when and how verbal and non-verbal activities can substitute for or complement each other, or whether they ever need to co-occur for unambiguous communication to be achieved. Perhaps it is out of relatively intensive studies of the interplay of such factors in relatively homogeneous conditions that general principles and their explanations may be developed. We should, presumably, be interested to know why the links found are as they are. The studies mentioned at the beginning of this chapter suggest, but in no way entail, that particular functions are typically realized mainly by features at particular levels of analysis.

Why should vocalic quality link with emotions rather than social identity or role relationships? Why should the articulation of particular phonemes be strong clues to social identity, while address forms chosen signal the nature of role relationships? Are these associations, if in fact they are genuine and general rather than artefacts of the interests of particular research workers, universal to mankind? If so, are some of the rather obvious explanations for each correct and sufficient?

In the meantime, it may be profitable to set the work reported into the more general methodological framework of the behavioural sciences and remind ourselves both about the goals of inquiry and the means most suitable for their pursuit. The intention is not to provide a three page summary of the philosophy of social psychology, but to note certain potential and actual sources of confusion and conflict and to see whether these are grounded in false premises. One problem encountered in any line of investigation is to know when to stop. To suggest that problems are satisfactorily solved or shelved is both true and false. Historically, these are fashionable topics, and 'language' is certainly *à la mode* at the present; and only a limited set of types of investigation are currently popular in this area. Some issues are resolved as a result of such empirical investigation and theoretical insight; but even when data are agreed and consensus attained on the acceptability of explanations, some worried and puzzled sceptic may always re-open the issues and expose the weaknesses. In this area there are limitations on what is possible that are rather different from those met with in the physical sciences, and it is important to bring these to mind periodically.

Limitations of the data

Our desires for precision of theory and delicacy of measurement must not be permitted to distort or exceed the qualities of the materials with which we are working. This proscription applies to both the social psychological and linguistic ends of the endeavour as much as to the intersection of the two. As we have mentioned at the beginnings of chapters 4, 5 and 6, distinctions between acute and chronic emotional states, chronic emotional states and personality traits, personality traits and interpersonal attitudes and role relationships are divisions of convenience without unambiguous boundaries. These are messy borders, only partially because we are slow to work out and agree upon appropriate taxonomies for attributes at different levels of analysis. When we do progress further, the levels of analysis and the classificatory systems at each level will remain hazy, because they are our constructed abstractions from phenomena which are not really discrete. The phenomena themselves are not necessarily amenable to the discovery or invention of cunning ways of achieving great fineness of measurement. We do not pretend to measure temperature on a ratio scale; neither do young chemists or physicists necessarily feel obliged to measure temperature to many places of decimals on any scale. The level of measurement is constrained by a sensible construction of the nature of the dimension and by the needs of the users, as well as by the availability of instrumentation. Botanists and zoologists find it useful to distinguish between species, genera, families, etc., without committing themselves to immutability, excessive purity or unequivocal criteria of identification within the categories. Similarly with social psychology and linguistics, while it is always appropriate to consider finer measurement techniques, categories and concepts, there is no need to spread data too thinly or squeeze it too hard. In fact it is a mistake to do so.

On the language side, we have noted, for instance, Austin's observation that performative utterances shade off into other sorts of utterance, and I suspect that he regretted that this was so. However, given that language is organic rather than mechanical, dynamic rather than static, then this is to be expected. In the future, we may wish to increase the range or use of performative verbs by extending the coverage of already available verbs or by introducing new meanings for others. The most obvious candidates for incorporation would be those verbs and structures already in the no-man's-land. As we institutionalize and bureaucratize behaviour, so we are liable to need verbal formulae to make acts explicit and public – and vice versa. At some point in time, we may prescribe a formula for a word like 'take' whereby 'I take this woman to be . . .' becomes, in appropriate contexts, a performative utterance with legal force. Similarly, we may wish to use a new formula 'I take this car . . .'. The word 'take' then achieves the status of a technical term with an unambiguous operationalized meaning in a defined context. This is a continuing process, both in everyday language and jargons specialized for limited purposes. Hence, at any one time we might expect some word units to fit clearly into categories, others to be way outside, and yet others hovering in the penumbra, with the possibility of moving in either direction, dependent upon subsequent consensus as to use.

This type of argument holds for the units and structures used for other functions of language. While the functions (and possibly their basic correlated structures, if any) may remain relatively constant, the particular exponents can change or be changed. The units and structures of a language can be adapted with greater or lesser success to meet the functions required of them. Some features remain constant: in any language there must be units which can be combined into patterns that have significance and meaning. As we have already stated, all natural languages extant actually employ several rather than only two layers of units, which has the economic consequence that fewer units are required at each level to achieve the same ultimate variety of messages. The abstraction of these layers has theoretical utility, but the categorizations within layers are not to be profitably pursued beyond certain limits. Any particular 'phoneme' of a language is a myth: individual speakers vary its pronunciation through time and with context, linguistic and otherwise; speakers from different geographical areas, social classes or ages will differ in their realizations and distributions of particular phonemes. Variety is the rule, not the exception. This does not, however, render the concept of 'phoneme' useless nor does it eliminate the possibility of a constructive study of the phonological system of a language. It means only that we should be careful not to demand or assume clearer boundaries and discriminations than the data themselves warrant.

Clearly the performative utterances mentioned could be studied further along those lines laid by Austin – and along others. Are the distinctions made by philosophers recognized, accepted and used by others users of the language? How do children come to learn that to say 'I promise' is to promise? Under what conditions do which people in fact deny the validity of performative utterances, and why? We could build up a social psychology of 'performatives', explicit and implicit, institutionalized and individualistic, ambiguous and unambiguous. We could also carry such an analysis over to other functions, particularly aspects of aesthetics, regulation of behaviour and affect of self and others, and expression of affect.

But we must not press too far, and we must allow for change. The adoption of this second attitude is sometimes seen by lay people and physical scientists as a frank admission of defeat, which it manifestly is not. It is not surprising that when a physicist gives some cunning interpretation of the behaviour of sub-atomic particles, these particles continue to follow the same laws of behaviour. They do not read the relevant reports, and they do not have aspirations to be something other than what they are. However, when a social psychologist exposes through the mass media how 'top people' behave, it is not surprising that aspirants to that category will attempt to modify their behaviour to come into line, while 'top people' themselves may modify theirs to ward off the potential invasion. We, as partially cognisant creatures, can adapt our behaviour in the light of knowledge about that behaviour. While it is true that in the short run we would expect only the particular exponents of regularities and explanations to change, but not the laws or theories themselves, in the long run these latter may change as well – adding zest to the game and ensuring employment for social scientists.

Related to this potential for change and the fuzziness of the border areas between the categories devised in psychology and linguistics, we may also note that language units themselves are *necessarily categorical*. One essential aspect of the system resides in its capacity for referring to objects, acts, attributes, and the relationships between these, with a finite number of units. To use a finite number of labels for referring to infinite variation entails abstraction and categorization. An item like 'table' necessarily ignores unique qualities of particular tables to achieve a contrast between one set of objects and others. The abstraction of what is common to a set with its categorizing verbal label, will focus upon some attributes rather than others. Once this has happened, it is easy to design or discover awkward instances that will not fit. To complain that a categorical system is categorical is to involve oneself in a misunderstanding of the system. The categories themselves are, hopefully, categories of convenience for reference and action in everyday discourse and are not designed for microscopic and inappropriate analysis. We have mentioned above the chimerical nature of the aims of transformational grammar and one reason for this arises from the simple, and in part trivial, fact that the categories of 'grammatical' and 'ungrammatical' can be thought of neither as totally non-overlapping or exhaustive, nor as peculiarly immune to change in definition.

Unfortunately, although these characteristics of the data save us from excessive meticulousness in our theory and measurement, they also present us with formidable empirical difficulties. The multivariate character of the phenomena of interest, in conjunction with the complexities of the decoding behaviour of receivers, renders experimentation difficult.

If all Hymes's SPEAKING variables are set at appropriate values, and the receiver is aware of the significance of these, an unambiguous message can be transmitted. Given that not all variables are so set, what is the receiver to do? It is possible that he will expect and need to be able to make a categorical judgement. His information is inadequate. Perhaps normally he would try to find out more before he makes an assessment. It is not very often, unfortunately, that we ask subjects how tentative their judgements are or what else they would like to know before deciding. For problems of marking attributes of speakers and role relationships, we would appear to be forced into rather large-scale experiments in which competent performers are required to systematically vary the values of all variables, while the experimenter observes how the nature of the receivers' judgements vary. While investigators like Argyle, Mehrabian and Triandis have begun to adopt such an approach, their stimulus presentations remain relatively unnatural, and they include only a few values of a few variables, with limited variations in subjects judging and being judged. Whether grand investigations are worth conducting is difficult to decide. It is probably the case that judges in fact treat only a small number of values as significant; possibly many variables could be discounted in that, if they were inappropriate, the judges would indicate the absurdity or impracticality of the experimenters' requests.

Most of the studies so far reported have been confined to the middle class sub-culture of two societies, the USA and the United Kingdom. The value of sound studies in other sub-cultures of these societies and cross-cultural studies of others is likely to be high.

Whatever social psychologists choose to explore further in these areas, there is little doubt that they will have to sharpen up their observational techniques and skills, devote more time to pains-taking participant observation, and improve the verisimilitude of their experimental materials and situations to extra-laboratory behaviour. The promotion-hunting, fund-raising, three-page publication relating x to y in situation z may be neatly controlled and quick and easy to conduct and analyse, but it will not answer the more important questions.

Objectives
Science and technology

Whether we use the terms 'science' and 'technology' or the other pair of modifiers to science, 'pure' and 'applied', we shall run the risk of being accused of making (or failing to make) value judgements. The intended contrast is between activities primarily orientated towards describing, explaining and understanding, and those directed towards using and controlling. There is no necessary, uncrossable divide separating the two, and mutual facilitation could be the most common mode of interaction. However, actual research projects often differ in their primary orientation, and people other than project directors are likely to have to play the synthesizing integrative roles. The contrast is worth drawing because, just as the appropriate basis for evaluating an utterance will shift from function to function of language, so legitimate criticism must differ according to the objectives of the research workers.

For example, clinically-orientated psychologists may successfully pin down those extra-, para-, and conventially linguistic features indicative of dispositional and reactive anxiety. This information may be used by practitioners in the exercise of their diagnostic and therapeutic roles. They need have no interest in why these features are associated with anxiety or any other state; the important thing may be to change the patient so that their incidence of occurrence drops. The same line of argument can be advanced, *mutatis mutandis*, for all applied problems involving verbal behaviour: getting children to dress themselves efficiently with self-generated verbal instructions;

generating prescriptions for address forms in a factory that will maximize job satisfaction and productivity; training the masses for mobility into the nobility; or devising educational systems which will prevent the majority of children from achieving intellectual maturity. Given a practicable objective, a technology can be accumulated. There are advantages to the pragmatic bias. It may well encourage the development of sound classificatory schemes. There will be a permanent concern for reliable and valid measurement. Success or failure will be evaluated periodically, if not continuously.

We may reasonably expect a continued growth in the number of studies associating social and verbal behaviour in applied settings where interested parties have to diagnose, change and monitor. The clinical, educational and industrial fields are the most likely immediate beneficiaries, but the accumulated data will have to be accounted for in theoretical frameworks. The work by Davitz on the identification of emotional states (chapter 4) is a good example of this kind of bias; Argyle's studies range across the chasm (chapter 5). (Is it an accident that both these sets of investigations show a persistent concern with the reliability of their data, which is not present in some of the more theoretically orientated work (e.g. Schegloff and Kendon in chapter 7)?)

On the pure science side, with its professed concern for understanding and explanation, the tendency is to move towards the more general and abstract, focusing on process and methodology rather than content and control. For example, there would tend to be relatively less interest in the formal linguistic structure of jokes and their differential funniness across different groups of people, and more in why some linguistic structures may be universally funny and others not. The perspective is likely to be concerned with understanding why verbal rather than non-verbal signalling systems are used for some functions rather than others – and vice versa. Schegloff's analysis of telephone conversations with its somewhat extended description of what is involved in 'Summoner: "Bill?"; Summoned: "What?"' (chapter 7), and Kendon's detailed analysis of role-switching in two conversations (chapter 7) exhibit this meticulous concern in very limited situations. The hope is that sufficient attention to particular cases may suggest very wide generalizations (just as the transformational generative approach examined specific, but carefully chosen, examples as problems whose resolution might throw up very general rules).

Those of more pragmatic bent are prone to be intolerant of the very abstract formulations derived from what are no more (and no less) than case-studies, but this is unwise. We cannot predict which bias is most likely to give the best pay-off in the short or long run. We have no grounds for supposing that a contract from the telecommunications industry or service, which requires its investigators to examine telephone conversations with a view to offering suggestions for ways of minimizing the time spent by users in identifying themselves and in getting on to the topic of the conversation, would provide us with a description and explanation of role-switching any faster or more effectively than the approach from pure science.

The simple conclusion is that it is regrettable if one line of work is viewed as obscure, pernickety and pedantic, and another is seen as atheoretical industrial cannon-fodder, when they might both be treated as legitimate enterprises of equally unknown efficacy. That the concern in this book has been on the pure science side is a fact (hopefully?) rather than a value judgement. If that has been the bias, what sort of descriptions and explanations are we seeking?

Are rules sufficient?

Ervin-Tripp (1969) emphasizes the importance of uncovering rules of substitution, co-occurrence and sequence. Hymes argues for:

... a study of speaking that seeks to determine the native system and theory of speaking; whose aim is to describe the communicative competence that enables a member of the community to know when to speak and when to remain silent, which code to use, when, where and to whom, etc. In considering what form socio-linguistic description might take, ... one needs to show sociologists, linguists and ethnographers and others a way to *see* data as the interaction of language and social setting (1967, p. 13).

Both these authors are advocating an approach which may have some similarity to the elaboration of derivational rules in transformational generative grammar. Ervin-Tripp would appear to be particularly enthusiastic about this pursuit, but we shall have to raise the question of whether this approach is likely to be profitable, if profitable whether sufficient, and if not, what might be done instead or as well.

The hunting of the linguistic universal in the studies of children's acquisition of mastery over the language system has opened up an old controversy in psychology in a new area. In the 1930s the dialectic raged around the 'learning' versus 'performance' controversy, but more recently the word 'competence' has been substituted for 'learning', and instead of the battle proceeding within psychology, it has criss-crossed the linguistics/psychology frontiers with some doubt as to who is fighting on which side at any one time. A caricature of the contrast would locate the linguist committed to the transformational camp as someone who is concerned to expose those rules by which grammatically acceptable sentences can be derived from kernel structures with invariable success, maximal parsimony, and elegance. He would concede that evidence can be collected from any source, but tends to find the informed opinions of himself and his colleagues a particularly useful criterion against which to validate the utterances that his ideas can be used to generate. It is this last preference that has led to charges of 'subjectivism', 'introspectionism' and 'rationalism'. None of these would seem to be valid, although the occasional child case study has led to the postulation of linguistic universals with a wild optimism (McNeill, 1966), subsequently modified (McNeill, 1970). The original introspectionists were behaving quite differently from Chomsky and his followers in that they were trying to observe their own thinking processes, which is not the same as discussing the grammaticality of sample sentences; always Chomsky and his sympathizers have worked with actual, even if constructed, sentences as a starting point. What is slightly worrying is that the distinction between legitimate means of generating data or ideas has not always been separated from the means of verifying ideas once promulgated. The proper testing of linguistic theory has not achieved the consensus on methodology that is found within psychology, so that, although criteria of evaluation can be specified, the means of application are less than obvious. The competence/performance issue becomes a central one as soon as someone asserts that linguistic theory is not concerned to describe and explain what is actually said by speakers, but what *could* be said without breaking rules. We may ignore a great deal of what has become a much more confusing issue than it need have done, but with the scene set for sociolinguists to model themselves on Chomsky's style, we must ask whether or not this is a wise choice.

An analogy may help, and games can once more do good service. If you wish to find out about chess, you will need to learn a number of things: the objective of the game and how it is realized, the rules governing the movements of individual pieces, and the rules governing taking turns and time-restrictions, if any. To ask an expert player about these features would be not only permissible, but intelligent. The prospect of watching a great number of matches with an inductive eye, to ascertain what can be found in a small booklet, seems unnecessarily tedious. When you have established this framework, you might wish to check its validity by playing games with other people, to see what happened when you moved pieces 'improperly' or yelled 'Check!' when it was not. (A similar procedure is in fact adopted by the linguist seeking to understand an unknown language with the help of an informant.) While such an analogy makes a travesty of the complexities of Chomsky's activities, it seems to me to be a fair representation of part of his procedure. He has not been interested in the objectives of the game, nor whether moves and sequences of moves are sensible or silly, but has sought to expose the rules which specify which piece can do what, etc. Take any particular game played and the application of appropriate rules would show whether it had been properly played. Once you have a means of generating movements, the application of the rules would also allow the generation of an infinite variety of games.

Such an analysis would not, however, explain games played in terms of sequences of moves. It would not help to make sense of the difference between the play of a Grand Master and an amateur. It would not help explain when and why rules are broken or why the entire set of pieces is sometimes swept on to the floor by an irate loser. It would not relate the moves to the objectives. These are questions that interest the behavioural scientists, both social and non-social psychologists. We need to know the rules of the game, but we want to know more as well.

Just as chess moves take on their meaning and significance in relation to the objective of checkmating, so with utterances and their functions. (Note that we can ask players about more than just the rules and receive useful answers without being intuitive, subjective or rationalist.) Some sequences are very complicated and, with built-in contingency plans, much more likely to result in victory than others. Some will be well known even to amateurs and can be easily identified, much as some speech correlates of emotional state or social identity can be readily detected. The analogy could be pursued *ad nauseam*, but for the moment it may suffice to say that social psychologists are as interested in games actually played as in games that might be played.

Transferring to language and social behaviour, we can first observe that the rules of the language game and the social game are not made available in simple booklet form and yet they are not totally obscure either. They may be vague and they may be kept hidden from others, but they can be discovered. When they are, we can go on to ask about people's behaviour in relation to these rules, observing the regularities and irregularities of their behaviour and eventually offer explanations of these as well. And we might hazard explanations for the rules taking the form they do.

In short, to expose the rules is but a prelude to the main business of relating language and social behaviour, a beginning not an end.

Means

In individual chapters, occasional suggestions have been thrown out for further investigation, but certain more general observations about the current state of the art can be made. Prescriptions offered are, of course, no more than personal prejudices, a fact which presumably constitutes no grounds for recommending or rejecting them. They refer mainly to techniques of study and data collection and to problems of description. Problems of explanation are virtually avoided.

In certain enterprises it is valuable to preface one's major efforts at resolving problems with periods of observation and/or rumination. Biologists, especially the ethological sub-species, are particularly prone to protracted periods of careful observation in the field before launching into experiments. Social psychologists often hasten into the neat but perhaps unnecessary manipulation. Work on social class is a case in point. People who have no first-hand experience of differences in life styles of different social groups are unlikely to come to understand the nature of the problems involved. Those who imagine the middle and upper classes have a little more money and the lower working class a little less and base their evaluations of theory purely on their examinations of data collected have not much chance of understanding the phenomena that are referred to in chapters 8 and 9. The point would be trite if it were not unfortunately so frequently ignored in the rush to get on with the experiments.

A similar stricture could be applied to those critics who would assert that Austin's analysis of performative utterances is trivial word chopping. Austin did not pretend to do more than conceptual wood-clearing. His activities had an essential similarity to those of the careful observer except that his personal accumulated knowledge was sufficient to generate his own data; he was working upon data he had already collected, not speculating upon invented utterances in an ivory tower. In one sense, he was exposing what the language can be made to do, rather than what it is generally used for. Which people are aware of and use the distinctions he draws, and why, are matters for systematic empirical investigation. But if you can understand and concur with the meaningfulness of the categories of his analysis then he may also have been showing how the language is used by some people – yourself and Austin to name but two.

Both these types of inquiry seem to be obvious and sensible preliminary stages in any endeavour to explore relationships between language and social behaviour.

Still considering ways of tackling problems, we can ask about the suitability of case-studies and surveys, naturalistic observation and experimentation. One disadvantage of highly detailed analyses of limited situations with small numbers of homogeneous participants is that the results and interpretations may not stand generalization. On the other hand, largescale investigations are liable to ride roughshod over individual or even group differences among subjects and over contexts. For example, grand counts of linguistic features used by five-year-olds across a range of contexts each explicitly intended to encourage rather different speech styles (narration, description, explanation) can obscure social class differences within contexts. Division by context can yield results (see Henderson, 1970b). Unless one has good theoretical or other grounds for choosing the grand design, it would seem safer to get to close grips with a strictly delimited problem using a homogeneous group of subjects – and then accumulate and collate both problems and subjects in the light of initial results and the ideas these suggest. It is worth repeating that, if there are general laws governing verbal behaviour and if they have explanations, they will be manifest with a few subjects as clearly as with many, and that a conservative piece-meal strategy is more likely to provide accumulative knowledge than a large-scale gamble. Thus, it is safer to focus on address forms (proper names and pronouns) as a clearly limited aspect of role relationships and work through their range of utility, than to include in one fell swoop all the verbal and non-verbal means that might be relevant. Brown achieved a similar, earlier success with this strategy when he promoted research into the value of the Whorfian hypothesis in application to colour words of the lexis (Brown and Lenneberg, 1954; Lantz and de Stefflre, 1964). Kendon's research strategy may prove similarly fruitful.

Related to this preference is a second, that observational situations and materials should be as natural as possible. Stimulus materials should be familiar to subjects, and their responses should not require strange discriminations or judgements. Judging emotional expressions of identikit pictures with a response array of emotion words outside the judges' normal usage is less likely to give information on how people make judgements than video-recordings where judges choose their own response terms and feel free not to pass any judgement – at least in the initial stages of inquiry. To ask a man on a Clapham omnibus whether he would call a bishop 'Your Grace' or 'Your Worship' may provide some strange answers, unless he numbers a bishop among his acquaintances. This complaint was made in chapter 5 about stereotypes. Similarly, if one is interested in cues for role switching in telephone conversations, experienced subjects have a greater appeal than naïve ones.

A subsidiary aspect of this problem would be the fineness of the scoring categories used. As we saw in chapter 6, Staples (1971) used five values of situation to examine how people's address forms changed with context. Her subjects appeared to use only three. A slightly finer scale than that actually used by the respondents is probably ideal more often than any other. Further, in chapter 5, we reported Labov's detailed analysis of the pronunciation of selected phonemes by New Yorkers of different classes in different situations. His results showed up differences detectable by the ear of a trained phonetician and merit interest to that extent. But could New York citizenry spot the differences and do they in their everyday encounters? If not, the distributions reported do not have social significance for common observers. Giles (1971c) used 'ordinary' respondents to see whether they could detect accent changes in subjects and they could. If we are interested in voice characteristics as markers used by receivers, Giles's procedure has advantages over Labov's. In fact we do not know whether Labov's analysis was beyond normal discriminatory behaviour, but it is possible that it was unnecessarily fine from that point of view.

Successive detailed analyses of behaviour of homogeneous sets of subjects in limited contexts, respondent-anchored scoring, and verisimilitude of experimental conditions will all exert pressures towards the development of satisfactory taxonomies. It is on the social psychological side that these are particularly weak. We cannot offer satisfactory classificatory systems of any of the states or behaviours mentioned: emotions, interpersonal attitudes, personality traits, social identities, role relationships, or encounters. The absence of sound description precludes the possibility of generally validated explanation, but still the gaps remain. The linguistic side is healthier within much of phonology and grammar. On the extra- and para-linguistic ends, attempts have been made to list possible variables, and prosodic features are at last receiving more attention now (e.g. Crystal, 1969). Lexis, while not accorded much interest, may not present great difficulties, but semantics and pragmatics do and will. Functions of language we have tried to attack, and hopefully some progress will be made with them in the not too distant future. It will, if the language in this book serves the function intended for it.

References

ANNETT, J. (1969), *Feedback and Human Behaviour*, Penguin Books.

ARGYLE, M. (1969), *Social Interaction*, Methuen.

ARGYLE, M. (1972), 'Non-verbal communication in human social interaction', in Hinde, R. (ed.), *Non-verbal Communication*, Cambridge University Press.

ARGYLE, M., ALKEMA, F., and GILMOUR, R. (1971), 'The communication of friendly and hostile attitudes by verbal and non-verbal signals', *Europ. J. soc. Psychol.*, vol. 2, pp. 385–402.

ARGYLE, M., and KENDON, A. (1967), 'The experimental analysis of social performance', *Adv. exp. soc. Psychol.*, vol. 3, pp. 55–98.

ARGYLE, M., and MCHENRY, R. (1971), 'Do spectacles really affect judgements of intelligence?', *Brit. J. soc. clin. Psychol.*, vol. 10, pp. 27–9.

ARGYLE, M., SALTER, V., NICHOLSON, H., WILLIAMS, M., and BURGESS, P. (1970), 'The communication of inferior and superior attitudes by verbal and non-verbal signals', *Brit. J. soc. clin. Psychol.*, vol. 9, pp. 222–31.

ASCH, S. E. (1952), *Social Psychology*, Prentice Hall.

ATKINSON, J. W. (1958), *Motives in Fantasy, Action, and Society*, Van Nostrand.

ATKINSON, J. W. (1964), *An Introduction to Motivation*, Van Nostrand.

AUSTIN, J. L. (1962), *How to Do Things with Words*, Oxford University Press.

AYER, A. J. (1936), *Language, Truth and Logic*, Gollancz.

BALES, R. F. (1950), *Interaction Process Analysis*, Addison-Wesley.

BALES, R. F. (1961), 'Task roles and social roles in problem-solving groups', in Maccoby, E. E., Newcomb, T. M., and Hartley, E. L. (eds.), *Readings in Social Psychology*, 3rd edn, Methuen.

BAVELAS, A. (1950), 'Communication patterns in task-oriented groups', *J. Acoust. Soc. Amer.*, vol. 22, pp. 725–30.

BERELSON, B. (1952), *Content Analysis in Communication Research*, Free Press.

BERLIN, B., and KAY, P. (1969), *Universality and Evolution of Basic Color Terms*, University of California Press.

BERNSTEIN, B. B. (1958), 'Some sociological determinants of perception', *Brit. J. Sociol.*, vol. 9, pp. 159–74.

BERNSTEIN, B. B. (1961), 'Social structure, language and learning', *Educ. Res.*, vol. 3, pp. 163–76.

BERNSTEIN, B. B. (1962a), 'Linguistic codes, hesitation phenomena and intelligence', *Language and Speech*, vol. 5, pp. 31–46.

BERNSTEIN, B. B. (1962b), 'Social class, linguistic codes, and grammatical elements', *Language and Speech*, vol. 5, pp. 221–40.

BERNSTEIN, B. B. (1970), 'A socio-linguistic approach to social learning', in Williams, F. (ed.), *Language and Poverty*, Markham.

BERNSTEIN, B. B., and BRANDIS, W. (1970), 'Social class differences in communication and control', in Brandis, W. and Henderson, D., *Social Class, Language and Communication*, Routledge & Kegan Paul.

BERNSTEIN, B. B., and HENDERSON, D. (1969), 'Social class differences in the relevance of language to socialization', *Sociology*, vol. 3, pp. 1–20.

BERNSTEIN, B. B., and YOUNG, D. (1967), 'Social class differences in conceptions of the uses of toys', *Sociology*, vol. 1, pp. 131–40.

BLOM, J. P., and GUMPERZ, J. J. (1972), 'Social meaning in linguistic structures: code switching in northern Norway', in Gumperz, J. J., and Hymes, D. (eds.), *Directions in Socio-linguistics*, Holt, Rinehart & Winston.

BOGARDUS, E. S. (1933), 'A social distance scale', *Sociol. soc. Res.*, vol. 17, pp. 265–71.

BOOMER, D. S. (1965), 'Hesitation and grammatical encoding', *Language and Speech*, vol. 8, pp. 148–58.

BRANDIS, W. (1970), 'An index of social class', in Brandis, W., and Henderson, D., *Social Class, Language and Communication*, Routledge & Kegan Paul, Appendix 1.

BRANDIS, W., and HENDERSON, D. (1970), *Social Class, Language and Communication*, Routledge & Kegan Paul.

BROWN, B. (1969), 'The social psychology of variations in French Canadian speech styles', Ph.D. thesis, McGill University, Montreal.

BROWN, R. (1965), *Social Psychology*, Collier-Macmillan.

BROWN, R., and BELLUGI, U. (1964), 'Three processes in the acquisition of syntax', *Harv. educ. Rev.*, vol. 34, pp. 133–51.

BROWN, R., and FORD, M. (1961), 'Address in American English', *J. abnorm. soc. Psychol.*, vol. 62, pp. 375–85.

BROWN, R., and GILMAN, A. (1960), 'The pronouns of solidarity and power', in Sebeok, T. A. (ed.), *Style in Language*, Wiley.

BROWN, R., and LENNEBERG, E. H. (1954), 'A study in language and cognition', *J. abnorm. soc. Psychol.*, vol. 49, pp. 454–62.

BRUNSWIK, E. (1956), *Perception and the Representative Design of Psychological Experiments*, University of California Press.

CARTER, L., HAYTHORN, W., MEIROWITZ, B., and LANZETTA, J. (1951), 'A note on a new technique of interaction recording', *J. abnorm. soc. Psychol.*, vol. 46, pp. 258–60.

CARTWRIGHT, D., and ZANDER, A. (1960) (eds.), *Group Dynamics*, 2nd edn, Tavistock.

CATTELL, R. B. (1957), *Personality and Motivation*, World Book Co.

CAZDEN, C. B. (1970), 'The neglected situation in child language research and education', in Williams, F. (ed.), *Language and Poverty*, Markham.

CENTRAL ADVISORY COUNCIL FOR EDUCATION (1967), *Children and their Primary Schools*, vol. 2. HMSO (*Plowden Report*).

CHEYNE, W. M. (1970), 'Stereotyped reactions to speakers with Scottish and English regional accents', *Brit. J. soc. clin. Psychol.*, vol. 9, pp. 77–9.

CHILD, I. L. (1969), 'Esthetics', in Lindzey, G., and Aronson, E. (eds.), *Handbook of Social Psychology*, vol. 3. Addison Wesley.

CHOMSKY, N. (1965), *Aspects of a Theory of Syntax*, MIT Press.

COLLINS, B. E., and GUETZKOW, H. (1964), *A Social Psychology of Group Processes for Decision-making*, Wiley.

COOK–GUMPERZ, J. (1973), *Social Control and Socialization*, Routledge & Kegan Paul.

COOK, M. (1971), 'The incidence of filled pauses in relation to part of speech', *Language and Speech*, vol. 14, pp. 135–40.

COULTHARD, M. C. (1969), 'A discussion of restricted and elaborated codes', *Educ. Rev.*, vol. 22, pp. 38–51.

CREED, C. D. (1972), 'Parameters of social interaction and speech variation', Ph.D. thesis, University of Southampton.

CRYSTAL, D. (1969), *Prosodic Systems and Intonation in English*, Cambridge University Press.

DAVITZ, J. L. (1964), *The Communication of Emotional Meaning*, McGraw-Hill.

DE CECCO, J. P. (1968), *The Psychology of Learning and Instruction* Prentice Hall.

DEUTSCH, M., LEVINSON, A., BROWN, B. R., and PEISACH, E. C (1967), 'Communication of information in the elementary school classroom', in Deutsch, M. (ed.), *The Disadvantaged Child*, Basic Books.

DIBNER, A. S. (1956), 'Cue-counting: a measure of anxiety in interviews', *J. consult. Psychol.*, vol. 20, pp. 475–8.

EDWARDS, A. L. (1957), *The Social Desirability Variable in Personality Assessment and Research*, Holt, Rinehart & Winston.

ERVIN-TRIPP, S. M. (1964), 'An analysis of the interaction of language, topic and listener', in Gumperz, J. J., and Hymes, D. (eds.), *The Ethnography of Communication*, *Amer. Anthropologist*, vol. 66(6), 2, 86–102.

ERVIN-TRIPP, S. M. (1969), 'Sociolinguistics', in Berkowitz, L. (ed.), *Advances in Experimental Social Psychology*, vol. 4, pp. 91–165.

208 References

ERVIN-TRIPP, S. M. (1971), 'An overview of theories of grammatical development', in Slobin, D. I. (ed.), *The Ontogenesis of Grammar*, Academic Press.

EYSENCK, H. J. (1957), *The Dynamics of Anxiety and Hysteria*, Routledge & Kegan Paul.

EYSENCK, H. J. (1964), *Crime and Personality*, Routledge & Kegan Paul.

FERGUSON, C. A. (1959), 'Diglossia', *Word*, vol. 15, pp. 325–40.

FISHMAN, J. A. (1968), *Bilingualism in the Barrio*, U.S. Dept of Health and Education, New York.

FLAVELL, J. H. (1968), *The Development of Role-taking Skills in Children*, Wiley.

FLOWER, F. D. (1966), *Language and Education*, Longman.

FLUGEL, J. C. (1954), 'Humor and laughter', in Lindzey, G. (ed.), *Handbook of Social Psychology*, vol. 2, Addison-Wesley.

FRENDER, R., BROWN, B. and LAMBERT, W. E. (1970), 'The role of speech characteristics in scholastic success', *Canad. J. behav. Sci.*, vol. 2, pp. 299–306.

FRIES, C. C. (1940), *American English Grammar*, Appleton-Century-Crofts.

FRIES, C. C. (1952), *The Structure of English*, Harcourt Brace & World.

FUNKENSTEIN, D. H. (1966), 'The physiology of fear and anger', in Coopersmith, S. (ed.), *Frontiers of Psychological Research* (readings from *Scientific American*). Freeman.

GARDNER, R. A., and GARDNER, B. T. (1969), 'Teaching sign language to a chimpanzee', *Science*, vol. 165, pp. 664–72.

GARDNER, R. C., and TAYLOR, D. M. (1968), 'Ethnic stereotypes: their effects on person perception', *Canad. J. Psychol.*, vol. 22, pp. 267–76.

GENERAL REGISTER OFFICE (1960), *Classification of Occupations*, HMSO.

GILES, H. (1970), 'Evaluative reactions to accents', *Educ. Rev.*, vol. 22, pp. 211–27.

GILES, H. (1971a), 'Ethnocentrism and the evaluation of accented speech', *Brit. J. soc. clin. Psychol.*, vol. 10, pp. 26–7.

GILES, H. (1971b), 'Patterns of evaluation in reactions to RP, South Welsh and Somerset accented speech', *Brit. J. soc. clin. Psychol.*, vol. 10, pp. 280–81.

GILES, H. (1972), 'The effect of stimulus mildness-broadness in the evaluation of accents', *Language and Speech*, vol. 15, pp. 262–9.

GOFFMAN, E. (1963), *Behaviour in Public Places*, Free Press.

GOLDMAN-EISLER, F. (1968), *Psycholinguistics*, Academic Press.

GOLEMBIEWSKI, R. T. (1962), *The Small Group*, University of Chicago Press.

GORMAN, T. P. (1971), 'Socio-linguistic implications of a choice of media on instruction', in Whiteley, W. H. (ed.), *Language Use and Social Change*, Oxford University Press.

HALL, J., and CARADOG JONES, D. (1950), 'Social grading of occupation', *Brit. J. Sociol.*, vol. 1, pp. 31–55.

HALLIDAY, M. A. K. (1961), 'Categories of the theory of grammar', *Word*, vol. 17, pp. 241–92.

HALLIDAY, M. A. K. (1969), 'Relevant Models of Language', *Educ. Rev.*, vol. 22, pp. 26–37.

HALLIDAY, M. A. K., McINTOSH, A., and STREVENS, P. D. (1964), *The Linguistic Sciences and Language Teaching*, Longmans.

HAWKINS, P. R. (1969), 'Social class, the nominal group and reference', *Language and Speech*, vol. 12, pp. 125–35.

HENDERSON, D. (1970a), 'Contextual specificity, discretion and cognitive specialization: with special reference to language', *Sociology*, vol. 4, pp. 311–37.

HENDERSON, D. (1970b), 'Social class differences in form class usage among five-year-old children', in Brandis, W., and Henderson, D., *Social Class, Language and Communication*, Routledge & Kegan Paul.

HESS, R. D., and SHIPMAN, V. C. (1965), 'Early experience and the socialization of cognitive modes in children', *Child Develop.*, vol. 36, pp. 860–86.

HESS, R. D., and SHIPMAN, V. C. (1967), 'Cognitive elements in maternal behavior', in Hill, J. P. (ed.), *Minnesota Symposium on Child Psychology*, vol. 1, University of Minnesota Press.

HOCKETT, C. F. (1958), *A Course in Modern Lingustics*, Macmillan Co.

HOLSTI, O. R. (1968), 'Content analysis', in Lindzey, G., and Aronson, E. (eds.), *Handbook of Social Psychology*, vol. 2, Addison-Wesley.

HUNT, R. G., and LIN, T. K. (1967), 'Accuracy of judgments of personal attributes from speech', *J. Pers. soc. Psychol.*, vol. 6, pp. 450–53.

HYMES, D. (1964), 'Towards ethnographics of communication', in Gumperz, J. J., and Hymes, D. (eds.), *The ethnography of communication, Amer. Anthropologist*, vol. 66(6), pp. 21–34.

HYMES, D. (1967), 'Models of the interaction of language and social setting', *J. soc. Issues*, vol. 23, pp. 8–28.

JAFFE, J., and FELDSTEIN, S. (1970), *Rhythms of Dialogue*, Academic Press.

JAKOBSON, R. (1960), 'Linguistics and poetics', in Sebeok, T. A. (ed.), *Style in Language*, Wiley.

JARVIS, P. E. (1964), 'The effect of self-administered verbal instructions on simple sensory-motor performance in children', University Microfilms Inc., Ann Arbor, Michigan, (64–9238).

JORDAN, C. (1972), 'The grammar of working and middle class children using elicited imitations', *Language and Speech*, vol. 15 (in press).

JOURARD, S. M. (1971), *Self Disclosure*, Wiley.

KANFER, F. H., PHILLIPS, J. S., MATARAZZO, J. D., and SASLOW, G. (1960), 'The experimental modification of interviewer content in standardized interviews', *J. consult. Psychol.*, vol. 24, pp. 528–36.

KASL, S. V., and MAHL, G. F. (1965), 'The relationship of disturbances and hesitations in spontaneous speech to anxiety', *J. Pers. soc. Psychol.*, vol. 1, pp. 425–33.

KATZ, J. J., and FODOR, F. A. (1963), 'The structure of a semantic theory', *Language*, vol. 39, pp. 170–210.

KELLOG, W. N. (1968), 'Communication and language in the home-raised chimpanzee', *Science*, vol. 162, pp. 423–7.

KENDON, A. (1967), 'Some functions of gaze direction in social interaction', *Acta Psychol.*, vol. 26, pp. 22–63.

KENDON, A. (1970), 'Some relationships between body motion and speech', in Siegman, A., and Pope, B. (eds.), *Studies in Dyadic Interaction*, Pergamon.

KLEIN, W. L. (1964), 'An investigation of the speech-for-self of children', Ph.D. thesis, University of Rochester.

KNOWER, F. H. (1941), 'Analysis of some experimental variations of simulated vocal expressions of the emotions', *J. soc. Psychol.*, vol. 14, pp. 369–72.

KOHLBERG, L. (1969), 'Stage and sequence: the cognitive-developmental approach to socialization', in Goslin, D. (ed.), *Handbook of Socialization Theory and Research*, Rand McNally.

KRASNER, L. (1961), 'Studies of the conditioning of verbal behaviour', in Saporta, S. (ed.), *Psycholinguistics*, Holt, Rinehart & Winston.

KUHN, T. S. (1962), *The Structure of Scientific Revolutions*, University of Chicago Press.

LABOV, W. (1966), *The Social Stratification of Speech in New York City*, Center for Applied Linguistics, Washington, D.C.

LABOV, W. (1970), 'The study of language in its social context', *Studium Generale*, vol. 23, pp. 30–87.

LaCIVITA, A. F., KEAN, J. M., and YAMAMOTO, K. (1966), 'Socio-economic status of children and acquisition of grammar', *J. educ. Res.*, vol. 60, pp. 71–4.

LAMBERT, W. E. (1967), 'A social psychology of bilingualism', *J. soc. Issues*, vol. 23, pp. 91–109.

LAMBERT, W. E., HODGSON, R. C., GARDNER, R. C., and FILLENBAUM, S. (1960), 'Evaluational reactions to spoken languages', *J. abnorm. soc. Psychol.*, vol. 60, pp. 44–51.

LANTZ, D., and DE STEFFLRE, V. (1964), 'Language and cognition revisited', *J. abnorm. soc. Psychol.*, vol. 69, pp. 472–81.

LAWTON, D. (1968), *Social Class, Language and Education*, Routledge & Kegan Paul.

LAY, C. H., and BURRON, B. F. (1968), 'Perception of the personality of the hesitant speaker', *Percept. mot. Skills.*, vol. 26, pp. 951–6.

LEAVITT, H. J. (1951), 'Some effects of certain communication patterns on group performance', *J. abnorm. soc. Psychol.*, vol. 46, pp. 38–50.

LIBERMAN, P. (1967), *Intonation, Perception and Language*, MIT Press.

LOBAN, W. D. (1963), *The Language of Elementary School Children*, National Council of Teachers of English, Champaign, Ill., Research Rept 1.

LURIA, A. R. (1961), *The Role of Speech in the Regulation of Normal and Abnormal Behavior*, Pergamon.

LYUBLINSKAYA, A. A. (1957), 'The development of children's speech and thought', in Simon, B. (ed.), *Psychology in the Soviet Union*, Routledge & Kegan Paul.

MACLAY, H., and OSGOOD, C. E. (1959), 'Hesitation phenomena and spontaneous English speech', *Word*, vol. 15, pp. 19–44.

MAHL, G. F. (1956a), ' "Normal" disturbances in spontaneous speech', *Amer. Psychologist*, vol. 11, pp. 390–94.

MAHL, G. F. (1956b), 'Disturbances and silences in the patient's speech in psychotherapy', *J. abnorm. soc. Psychol.*, vol. 53, pp. 1–15.

MAHL, G. F. (1963), 'The lexical and linguistic levels in the expression of the emotions', in Knapp, P. H. (ed.), *Expression of the Emotions in Man*, International Universities Press.

MARKEL, N., and ROBIN, G. (1965), 'The effect of content and sex of judge on judgment of personality from voice', *Inter. J. soc. Psychiat.*, vol. 11, pp. 295–300.

MEHRABIAN, A. (1968), 'The inference of attitudes from the posture, orientation and distance of a communicator', *J. consult. Psychol.*, vol. 32, pp. 296–308.

MEHRABIAN, A., and DIAMOND, S. G. (1971), 'Seating arrangement and conversation', *Sociometry*, vol. 34, pp. 281–9.

MORRIS, C. (1946), *Signs, Language and Behaviour*, Prentice Hall.

MOSCOVICI, S. (1967), 'Communication processes and the properties of language', *Adv. exp. soc. Psychol.*, vol. 3, pp. 225–70.

MURRAY, H. A. (1938), *Explorations in Personality*, Oxford University Press.

MCCARTHY, J. J., and KIRK, S. A. (1961), *Illinois Test of Psycho-linguistic Abilities*, University of Illinois Press.

MCDOUGALL, W. (1908), *An Introduction to Social Psychology*, Luce.

MCNEILL, D. (1966), 'The creation of language by children', in Lyons, J., and Wales, R. (eds.), *Psycholinguistic Papers*, Edinburgh University Press.

MCNEILL, D. (1970), *The Acquisition of Language*, Harper & Row.

MCWIRTER, N. and MCWIRTER, R. (1970), *Guinness Book of Records*, Guinness Superlatives.

NEWSON, J. and NEWSON, E. (1970), *Four Years Old in an Urban Community*, Penguin Books.

OSGOOD, C. E. (1953), *Method and Theory in Experimental Psychology*, Oxford University Press.

OSGOOD, C. E. (1966), 'Dimensionality of the semantic space for communication via facial expression', *Scand. J. Psychol.*, vol. 7, pp. 1–30.

OSGOOD, C. E., SUCI, G. J., and TANNENBAUM, P. H. (1957), *The Measurement of Meaning*, University of Illinois Press.

OSGOOD, C. E., and WALKER, E. G. (1959), 'Motivation and language behaviour: a content analysis of suicide notes', *J. abnorm. soc. Psychol.*, vol. 59, pp. 58–67.

PEISACH. E. C. (1965), 'Children's comprehension of teacher and peer speech', *Child Develop.*, vol. 36, pp. 467–80.

PREMACK, D. (1970), 'The education of Sarah', *New Society*, vol. 422, pp. 768–71.

POOL, I. (1959), *Trends in Content Analysis*, University of Illinois Press.

QUILLIAN, M. R. (1966), *Semantic Memory*, Airforce Cambridge Research Laboratory, Bedford, Mass., Contr. No. A F 19 (628)-5065, Proj. 8668.

RACKSTRAW, S. J., and ROBINSON, W. P. (1967), 'Social and psychological factors related to variability of answering behaviour in five year old children', *Language and Speech*, vol. 10, pp. 88–106.

ROBINSON, W. P. (1965a), 'Cloze procedure as a technique for the investigation of social class differences in language usage', *Language and Speech*, vol. 8, pp. 42–55.

ROBINSON, W. P. (1965b), 'The elaborated code in working class', *Language and Speech*, vol. 8, pp. 243–52.

ROBINSON, W. P. (1973), 'Where do children's answers come from?', in Bernstein, B. (ed.), *Class, Codes and Control*, vol. 2, Routledge & Kegan Paul.

ROBINSON, W. P., and RACKSTRAW, S. J. (1967), 'Variations in mothers' answers to children's questions', *Sociology*, vol. 1, pp. 259–79.

ROBINSON, W. P., and RACKSTRAW, S. J. (1972), *A Question of Answers*, Routledge & Kegan Paul.

ROCKSBOROUGH-SMITH, N. (1968), 'Lexical redundancies in speech', unpublished M S, University of Southampton.

RUSSELL, B. (1912), *The Problems of Philosophy*, Home University Library.

SCHACHTER, S., and SINGER, J. E. (1962), 'Cognitive, social, and physiological determinants of emotional state', *Psychol. Rev.*, vol. 69, pp. 379–99.

SCHATZMAN, L., and STRAUSS, A. (1955), 'Social class and modes of communication', *Amer. J. Sociol.*, vol. 60, pp. 329–38.

SCHEGLOFF, E. A. (1968), 'Sequencing in conversational openings', *Amer. Anthropologist*, vol. 70, pp. 1075–95.

SCOTT, W. A. (1968), 'Attitude measurement', in Lindzey. G., and Aronson, E. (eds.), *Handbook of Social Psychology*, vol. 2, Addison-Wesley.

SEBEOK, T. A. (1960) (ed.), *Style in Language*, Wiley.

SELIGMAN, C. R., TUCKER, G. R., and LAMBERT, W. E. (1970), 'The effects of speech style on teachers' attitudes toward pupils', unpublished MS, McGill University, Montreal.

SHERIF, M. (1936), *The Psychology of Social Norms*, Harper & Row.

SHRINER, T. H., and MINER, L. (1968), 'Morphological structures in the language of disadvantaged and advantaged children', *J. speech and hearing Res.*, vol. 11, pp. 605–10.

SIEGMAN, A. W., and POPE, B. (1965), 'Effects of question specificity and anxiety producing messages on verbal fluency in the initial interview', *J. Pers. soc. Psychol.*, vol. 2, pp. 522–30.

SLOBIN, D. I. (1971), *The Ontogenesis of Grammar*, Academic Press.

SLOBIN, D. I., MILLER, S. H., and PORTER, L. W. (1968), 'Forms of address and social relations in a business organization', *J. Pers. soc. Psychol.*, vol. 8, pp. 289–93.

SOMMER, R. (1969), *Personal Space*, Prentice Hall.

SOSKIN, W. F., and JOHN, V. (1963), 'The study of spontaneous talk', in Barker, R. G. (ed.), *The Stream of Behaviour*, Appleton-Century-Crofts.

SPENCER, J. (1958), 'RP – some problems of interpretation', *Lingua*, vol. 7, pp. 7–29.

STAPLES, L. M. (1971), 'A study of address forms used in an hierarchical organization', unpublished MS, University of Southampton.

STAPLES, L. M., and ROBINSON, W. P. (1974), 'Address forms used by members of a department store', *Brit. J. soc. clin. Psychol.*, vol. 13, pp. 1–11.

STRONGMAN, K., and WOOZLEY, J. (1967), 'Stereotyped reactions to regional accents', *Brit. J. soc. clin. Psychol.*, vol. 6, pp. 164–7.

TAYLOR, W. L. (1953), ' "Cloze procedure": a new tool for measuring readability', *Journalism Quarterly*, vol. 30, pp. 415–33.

THOULESS, R. (1953), *Straight and Crooked Thinking*, Pan.

TRIANDIS, H. C., LOH, W. D., and LEVIN, L. A. (1966), 'Race, status, quality of spoken English and opinions about civil rights as determinants of interpersonal attitudes', *J. Pers. soc. Psychol.*, vol. 3, pp. 468–72.

TURNER, G. J. (1973), 'Social class and children's language of control at ages five and seven', in Bernstein, B. (ed.), *Class, Codes and Control*, vol. 2, Routledge & Kegan Paul.

TURNER, G. J., and MOHAN, B. A. (1970), *A Linguistic Description and Computer Program for Children's Speech*, Routledge & Kegan Paul.

UHLENBECK, E. M. (1970), 'The use of respect forms in Javanese', in Wurm, S. A., and Laycock, D. C. (eds.), *Pacific Linguistic Studies in Honour of Arthur Capell*, Pacific Linguistics, Sydney.

VETTER, H. J. (1969), *Language Behaviour and Psychopathology*, Rand McNally.

WARR, P. B., FAUST, J., and HARRISON, G. J. (1967), 'A British ethnocentrism scale', *Brit. J. soc. clin. Psychol.*, vol. 6, pp. 267–77.

WHORF, B. L. (1956), *Language. Thought and Reality*, MIT Press.

WILKINSON, A. (1965), 'Spoken English', *Educ. Rev.*, Suppl. to vol. 17, Occasional publ. 12.

WILLIAMS, F., and NAREMORE, R. C. (1969), 'On the functional analysis of social class differences in modes of speech', *Speech Monogr.*, vol. 36, pp. 77–102.

WILLIAMS, F., and WOOD, B. S. (1970), 'Negro children's speech: some social class differences in word predictability', *Language and Speech*, vol. 13, pp. 141–50.

WITTGENSTEIN, L. (1951), *Philosophical Investigations*, Blackwell.

Index